ALL THE GALLANT MEN

AN AMERICAN SAILOR'S FIRSTHAND ACCOUNT
OF PEARL HARBOR

DONALD STRATTON

WITH KEN GIRE

WILLIAM MORROW
An Imprint of HarperCollinsPublishers

Title page photograph by Ray Sandla. Unless otherwise noted, interior photographs are courtesy of the author.

HarperCollins books may be purchased for educational, business, or sales promotional use. For information, please email the Special Markets Department at SPsales@harpercollins.com.

FIRST EDITION

Part One image credit Naval Historical Foundation.
Part Two image credit U.S. Naval History and Heritage Command.
Part Three image credit Ray Sandla.
Maps on pages 84 and 90 credit Naval Historical Center.

Library of Congress Cataloging-in-Publication Data has been applied for.

ISBN 978-0-06-264535-7

16 17 18 19 20   DIX/RRD   10 9 8 7 6

If men could learn from history, what lessons it might teach us!
But passion and party blind our eyes, and the light which experience gives us
is a lantern on the stern which shines only on the waves behind.

—Samuel Taylor Coleridge

Contents

Part Three

ALL THE GALLANT MEN

Prologue

The Awakening

"I fear all we have done is to awaken a sleeping giant and fill him with a terrible resolve."
—Admiral Isoroku Yamamoto
Commander of Japan's Naval Forces

On the afternoon of December 7, 1941, news of the Japanese attack on Pearl Harbor, Hawaii, reached Washington, D.C. Rumors raced unchecked through the corridors of power. *The Pacific Fleet, destroyed? The island of Oahu, overrun? Japanese subs, seen off the coast of San Francisco? Japanese troops, mounting an amphibious landing? Japanese spies, living among us?*

Switchboards lit up; teletypes chattered. Presses were stopped, broadcasts interrupted.

The West Coast, with its large population of Japanese immigrants, panicked. Schools in California closed. So did businesses. "Extra!" editions of newspapers sold out as soon as their bundles hit the streets. And suddenly every Japanese-American living here was looked on with suspicion. Some were shunned. Others were harassed. And many, before the war's end, would be displaced, forced to live in internment camps.

As facts were checked and rumors dispelled, shock gave way to the sobering reality that America would be going to war—joining a global conflict it had wanted no part of. From coast to coast, people huddled around their radios, waiting to hear from their president. His "fireside chats" had gotten them through the Depression. If ever they needed a word from him, it was now.

The president's two speechwriters were out of town at the time, and so it would be his words, and only his, that the nation would hear. On the evening of December 7, President Franklin Delano Roosevelt called his secretary Grace Tully into his office. "Sit down, Grace. I'm going before Congress tomorrow, and I'd like to dictate my message. It will be short."

By midnight, he had finished. When he awoke the next morning, a typed draft was waiting for him. He went over the speech and dressed for the day.

At noon on December 8, Congress opened a special joint session with a prayer by the Senate chaplain, who called for national unity.

About that time, six limousines pulled up to the White House. Roosevelt walked to the presidential car, silent and somber, pushing his legs, clad in painful braces hidden under his suit. The door of the Cadillac opened, and he eased himself in. Outside his car stood six Secret Service agents, three to each running board, each holstering a .38-caliber revolver. Inside sat four more, with sawed-off shotguns. Security had been ratcheted up all around the capital, not just for the president. Tensions were high. Everyone was wary.

Inside the car the president was poring over his speech, weighing every word. His opening line announced that the previous day would "live in history." It now seemed too pale a phrase. He scratched out "history." He needed something ruddier, flushed with outrage.

Above it, he printed the perfect word—"infamy."

At 12:20, the president's motorcade pulled into the parking lot of the U.S. Capitol. When the somber procession stopped, Roosevelt emerged from his limousine, wearing a navy blue cape over his shoulders. His son James was a captain in the Marine Corps and was wearing his dress blue uniform as he took his place at his father's side.

His arm steadied his father as they made their way to the House chamber. The room was packed with senators, representatives, justices of the Supreme Court, and members of the president's cabinet, along with the highest-ranking military leaders. His wife of thirty-six years, Eleanor Roosevelt, watched from the upstairs gallery, which was filled to capacity with more than five hundred people eagerly waiting for the president to speak.

The entire nation was an extension of that audience, gathering around radios. In Red Cloud, Nebraska, my family collected before a wooden, battery-operated radio that sat on a windowsill in the living room for better reception. It was now 12:30 P.M., and the gears of commerce halted, not just in tiny Red Cloud but in every town and city where those radio waves reached.

When all were seated, the Speaker of the House, Sam Rayburn, announced: "The President of the United States." The cavernous chamber erupted in cheers and applause. Still steadied by the arm of his son, the president walked the aisle, giving no greetings, shaking no hands, offering no smiles. He stepped onto the ramp to the podium, one measured step after another. As the cheers and applause reached a crescendo, even Roosevelt's most strident opponents were wiping tears from their eyes.

An American flag hung vertically behind the dais, framing the president. An expectant hush fell over the room. He placed on the podium a black, loose-leaf, schoolboy's notebook that held fewer than three pages of words. He spoke without gestures. His voice was clear. His language, measured. His tone, resolute. And just behind his words burned the anger of a nation that had been so violently awakened.

Mr. Vice President, Mr. Speaker, Members of the Senate, and of the House of Representatives.

Yesterday, December 7th, 1941—a date that will live in infamy—the United States of America was suddenly and deliberately attacked by naval and air forces of the Empire of Japan.

The United States was at peace with that nation and, at the solicitation of Japan, was still in conversation with its government and its emperor looking toward the maintenance of peace in the Pacific.

Indeed, one hour after Japanese air squadrons had commenced bombing in the American island of Oahu, the Japanese ambassador to the United States and his colleague delivered to our Secretary of State a formal reply to a recent American message. And while this reply stated that it seemed useless to continue the existing diplomatic negotiations, it contained no threat or hint of war or of armed attack.

It will be recorded that the distance of Hawaii from Japan makes it obvious that the attack was deliberately planned many days or even weeks ago. During the intervening time, the Japanese government has deliberately sought to deceive the United States by false statements and expressions of hope for continued peace.

The attack yesterday on the Hawaiian Islands has caused severe damage to American naval and military forces. I regret to tell you that very many American lives have been lost. In addition, American ships have been reported torpedoed on the high seas between San Francisco and Honolulu.

Yesterday, the Japanese government also launched an attack against Malaya.

Last night, Japanese forces attacked Hong Kong.

Last night, Japanese forces attacked Guam.

Last night, Japanese forces attacked the Philippine Islands.

Last night, the Japanese attacked Wake Island.

And this morning, the Japanese attacked Midway Island.

Japan has, therefore, undertaken a surprise offensive extending throughout the Pacific area. The facts of yesterday and today speak for themselves. The people of the United States have already formed their opinions and well understand the implications to the very life and safety of our nation.

As Commander in Chief of the Army and Navy, I have directed that all measures be taken for our defense. But always will our whole nation remember the character of the onslaught against us.

No matter how long it may take us to overcome this premeditated invasion, the American people in their righteous might will win through absolute victory.

I believe that I interpret the will of the Congress and of the people when I assert that we will not only defend ourselves to the uttermost, but will make it very certain that this form of treachery shall never again endanger us.

Hostilities exist. There is no blinking at the fact that our people, our territory, and our interests are in grave danger.

With confidence in our armed forces, with the unbounding determination of our people, we will gain the inevitable triumph—so help us God.

I ask that the Congress declare that since the unprovoked and dastardly attack by Japan on Sunday, December 7th, 1941, a state of war has existed between the United States and the Japanese empire.

The joint session leapt to its feet as one, thundering its applause. A short debate followed, then the resolution was put to a vote.

It passed the Senate, 82–0.

The House, 388–1.

In the six and a half minutes it took for the president to deliver his address, the nation was shaken from its isolationism and roused to its feet to join the greatest armed conflict in human history, a fight in which the fate of the world would be determined. The speech not only traveled over the airwaves of our nation, it circled the globe, giving hope to every war-torn country engaged in the awful bloodletting that would come to be known as the Second World War. And yet, as the president's words faded, the outcome of the coming battle was far from ordained: Imperial Japan and Nazi Germany had raced almost unchecked across Asia and Europe; the holdouts, Britain, Russia, and China, were on the brink. The United States faced one of the greatest tests of its life.

As AMERICA RALLIED around the president's words and prepared for the coming battles, the war already had come to my fellow shipmates and me. Without debate, without discussion, without formal declaration. It arrived at dawn, without warning. It swooped down ruthlessly and relentlessly, one squadron after another after another. Worst of all, it came *gleefully*, the Japanese pilots taunting us as they passed, smiling at us, waving to us, laughing at us.

I was aboard the USS *Arizona* on the morning of December 7, 1941. The courage I saw in our men was astonishing. Those gallant sailors fought back however they could. Pilots tried to locate airplanes that were still operable, but only a few managed to get in the air and into the fight. Gunners found themselves with only the ammunition in their ready boxes, with the rest of the munitions they so desperately needed locked up belowdecks. If the bullets ran out, they raced to another gun, often one that had a fallen sailor crumpled beneath it. The rest of the men fought back with whatever weapons were at hand, shooting at the streaking Japanese Zeros with lightweight machine guns, rifles, even pistols.

Acts of individual heroism could be witnessed everywhere

you looked. Men being strafed as they brought boxes of ammo up ladders to the antiaircraft guns. Other men carrying their wounded buddies to safety, trying desperately to stanch their bleeding. Still others in small boats, navigating through the fiery sea, pulling oil-soaked sailors from the water. Many putting out fires on board their ships. All the while these men were dodging enemy bullets that were cutting everything around them to shreds, including their fellow sailors.

WE WERE NOT extraordinary men, those of us who fought on that infamous date in December seventy-five years ago. Truth be told, most of us had enlisted because there were precious few jobs to be found where we lived. The Great Depression had pulled the pockets of the economy inside out, leaving little more than a lint's worth of hope for the young men entering the workforce. Most of us who enlisted did so because we needed a job.

Pearl Harbor changed that. A surge of patriotism swept the country, and everyone threw themselves into the war effort. Love for country welled up inside seemingly every American, coming out in the songs we sang, in the movies produced, in the newspaper articles that were written. We were ordinary men. What was extraordinary was the country we loved. We loved who she was, what she stood for. We loved her for what she meant to us, and for what she had given to us, even in those meager times. It didn't matter where you hailed from, whether you came from the mountains or the prairies, a sprawling city or a small coastal town: you loved her. We all did—more than the states we left behind, our homes, the careers we gave up. As too many would prove, we loved her more than our very lives.

The battleships and destroyers at Pearl Harbor were named after states from where some of us had been raised. Ohio. Tennessee. Oklahoma. Maryland. California. West Virginia. Utah. Nevada. Those vessels moored in that harbor so far from home reminded us where we came from.

The battleship I served my country on was the USS *Arizona*.

The men on that ship were drawn from different parts of the country. Some came from family farms in the Midwest. Some were fresh from the steel mills of Chicago. Others joined from dirt-poor towns in the Deep South. A few arrived with book smarts from places foreign to the rest of us—Annapolis, Notre Dame, Vanderbilt. They came from different religious backgrounds. Some were Catholics, some Protestants, some Jews. Others weren't sure what they were. A few didn't care. After all, many were still teenagers with their whole lives stretching before them. There would be plenty of time for religion, later. They came from different ethnic backgrounds, too. Their accents betrayed them.

There was a Jastrzemski from Michigan.

An O'Bryan from Massachusetts.

A Schroeder from New Jersey.

A Giovenazzo from Illinois.

A Riggins from California.

A Nelson from Arkansas.

A Smith from just about everywhere—Virginia, Missouri, Florida, Illinois, California, Ohio, Tennessee, Arkansas, Texas, Oklahoma, Mississippi.

And a Stratton from Nebraska.

What happened on December 7, 1941, if it didn't kill us, changed us forever. President Roosevelt was right to call it "a date that will live in infamy." But for my fellow survivors and me, it also is alive in memory, like shrapnel left embedded in our brains because the surgeon thought it too dangerous to operate. Those images remain with us survivors seventy-five years later. Sometimes they intrude into our day, a moment spontaneously combusting, and suddenly we are back in the flames that engulfed our ship or in the oil-slick waters that surrounded it. Sometimes they come to us in the night, a haunt of images that troubles our sleep. Or perhaps the phone rings, and we flinch. Or a car backfires, and instinctively we duck.

These memories lie within me, forever still and silent, like the men entombed in the *Arizona*. Others, like the oil that seeps from its wreckage, slip around inside me until they find a way out and make their way to the surface, where they pool and sometimes catch fire.

OVER THE YEARS, many of us made the pilgrimage back to that harbor, where we have experienced both the soothing of those wounds, and, at the same time, a reopening of them. Have some been healed? Yes. Year by merciful year. But *all?* No. And that is true for so many who have survived trauma, not just those who have survived the horror of war.

With each anniversary our ranks thin.

Three hundred thirty-five *Arizona* sailors survived that day. Only five remain.

I am looking forward to reuniting with them on the seventy-fifth anniversary of Pearl Harbor in December 2016. Realistically, though, I realize I am about out of anniversaries. At ninety-four, I don't take the years ahead for granted. Not one.

More than 65 percent of my body was burned in the explosion that sank the *Arizona*. My body is a patchwork of scars and skin grafts. Much of the feeling has come back. But not all. My joints are stiff, and I have to push myself up from my chair, then steady myself before I take the first tentative step.

It's been said that when an old person dies, it is like a library burning down. Having survived a fire that took so much from me, I have an obligation to save what memories I have from the flames that will one day come and claim what is left of me.

I share what I remember when I can. But a day will come when I can no longer speak. *What then?* I have asked myself. *What will become of the memories that I as a survivor have experienced? Or the lessons that we as a nation have learned?*

That is why I wrote this book.

I wanted to save from the fire something of my memories of the *Arizona* so that younger generations, and all of the children to come after them, can understand why Pearl Harbor matters. Though my memory is pretty good, here and there I have needed to augment it with research, and I am indebted to those sources that helped clarify my recollections. Most of the memories are my own, but I didn't want the story to be exclusively mine. It's important to me that the experiences of my shipmates and of other sailors, soldiers, and Marines who fought that day be included. They deserve to be heard, even though they are gone.

Especially because they are gone.

PART ONE

1

A Child of the Depression

Men stood by their fences and looked at the ruined corn, drying fast now, only a little green showing through the film of dust. The men were silent and they did not move often. And the women came out of the houses to stand beside their men—to feel whether this time the men would break. The women studied the men's faces secretly, for the corn could go, as long as something else remained. The children stood near by, drawing figures in the dust with bare toes, and the children sent exploring senses out to see whether men and women would break.

—John Steinbeck,
The Grapes of Wrath

What I saw that December morning in 1941, what all of us survivors witnessed, was the stuff of nightmares. When the living go back to walk among the dead, even in memory, it comes at a price. Can I afford it? I wonder. Can I keep going back there—to that day, to those images?

I wear to this day the physical scars from that attack, never letting me forget that terrible date. But, like the rest of those who survived that day, I have other wounds, ones that can't be covered up with slacks and long-sleeved shirts. Scars on a part of me no one can see.

I wasn't always like that.

I was once just a boy from Nebraska.

I grew up the son of a corn husker who lost all he had in the Dust Bowl and the Great Depression. He didn't have much, so he didn't have much to lose. But there were other, deeper losses he incurred, more devastating than the cost of anything material. His dreams, small as they were, were gone. Much of who he was and thought he might become, crumbled. That agonizingly long decade was like a biblical plague of locusts that swarmed down on the small cornfield that was his life, stripping those things from him. From all of us.

The 1,512 sailors on the *Arizona* came out of those years, along with all the other men who fought in World War II. The Depression was the forge that formed us. When the fight came to us, we were ready for it. Like steel coming out of the blast furnaces, shaped into girders, then dipped into vats of oil to temper them. There was a strength you couldn't see on the surface. Because of it, we were somehow able to bear the weight that a world at war placed on our shoulders.

I didn't know I had it in me, some of the things the war brought out. I don't think any of us did—you never know the strength of steel until it is tested.

Even so.

We were so young, those of us who enlisted—eighteen, nineteen, twenty years old. Too young to go through what we endured that day, I can tell you that. If we were not quite men on December 6, by midmorning of the 7th we were.

This is my story. It is just one of thousands from those who shared that fateful day. And only one of hundreds of thousands from other sailors, soldiers, and airmen who joined the fight in the fateful days that followed. But it was mine to live, that story. And now, I figure, it is time to tell it.

I WAS BORN July 14, 1922, to Robert J. Stratton and Jesse Ray Rutledge. We lived on a farm that wasn't ours, in a community that wasn't large enough to qualify as a town. Barely a dot in the middle of the Great Plains, Inavale, Nebraska, was a crosshatch of dirt roads with a few tumbledown houses, none of which had electricity or running water.

While those in big cities were experiencing the frothy excesses of the Roaring Twenties, we in rural America were working our fingers to the bone, eking out a living. That's what my father did. He was a sharecropper, finding whatever work he could to provide for his family. My mother bore him four children. I was the oldest. I shared a room with my two younger brothers, Darrel and William, while my sister Norma slept in my parents' bedroom. My parents worked from can to can't, fixing all six of our meals, washing all six of our clothes, mending and patching them, making do while somehow making a life for all six of us, and holding that life together.

As the 1920s passed into the 1930s, the farms that fanned out from Inavale eventually gave out. One by one, banks foreclosed on them, leaving them derelict. Or their tenants simply packed up what little they had and left them to the dust that had collected in drifts along the fence lines.

Few bothered to chronicle the despair. Timothy Egan, author of *The Worst Hard Time*, explores why:

The land convulsed in a way that had never been seen before, and it did so at a time when one out of every four adults was out of work. The people who live here now, the ones who never left, are still trying to make sense of why the earth turned on them. Much as they love this place, their doubts run deep. Was it a mistake to hang on? Will they be the last generation to inhabit the southern plains? And some felt deep shame—for the land's failure, and their part in it. Outside Invale not long ago, an old woman was found burning a Dust Bowl diary written by her husband. Her neighbor was astonished: why destroy such an intimate family record? The horror, the woman explained, was not worth sharing. She wanted it gone forever.

Most tenants went west. My family headed east, a few miles down the road to Red Cloud, which was midway on Nebraska's southern border. I was nine when we got there. Unlike Inavale, Red Cloud was a proper town. Founded in 1871, it was named after the great Plains Indian chief, a Lakota Sioux who three years earlier had made peace with the United States after a bloody war that also bears his name. By the 1930s the town had 1,500 people, a couple of grocery stores, a post office, retail stores, a school system, and a handful of churches. Most of the residents were Lutherans, but there was a fair number of Baptists, Methodists, and Catholics. Mom was the religious one in the family, a Methodist. That was *her* church, and, by extension, it became ours.

What I recall from my place on a hard wooden pew in that little Methodist church was not so much what I heard from the pulpit as what I saw in the people. Hardscrabble farmers in their hand-sewn Sunday best with starched collars chafing their necks. Their wives sitting next to them, dressed in faded floral prints. Next to them squirmed uneven rows of free-range children, trying their best to sit still and "be reverent." They were dressed in hand-me-downs that had been soaked in outdoor tubs, scrubbed on wooden washboards, and pressed with irons heated on stovetops. The girls smelled of their mothers' rosewater; the boys, of their fathers' hair oil.

When the offering plate was passed, I watched it make its way down one pew and up another, hearing the clink of coins as the small, clutched hands of those children dropped their offerings into the plate. Most of the families in that church had little to live on and nothing to spare, yet somehow the parents found nickels and dimes for their children to give.

I remember how the church people came together to help whenever one of those farmers needed it, whenever one of those mothers gave birth, whenever one of those children fell sick, or whenever one of them died. I remember the funerals, the food people brought, how they showed up and pitched in, and how the grief was somehow made bearable because a family didn't have to shoulder it alone.

I remember "The Lord's Supper" and the hush that came over everyone when it was Communion Sunday. I didn't understand the "take-and-eat" mystery of it all, but I came to understand the sacrifice that had been made and the importance of honoring that sacrifice by remembering it.

When we went to church, we walked, all six of us. Mom made sure we washed the night before, that we were up early, our faces washed, our hair brushed, our fingernails clipped. At night, I would often see her read our big family Bible. In the morning, if I was up early, I would sometimes see her on her knees, praying. In the hours between, she might quote a Bible verse as a reminder of what was expected of us. She was never harsh. She would just say something like, "Do you think Jesus would approve of that, Donny?" Or when we would run out of something, she would tell us not to worry. "The good Lord" would take care of it, she assured us. Her theology was simple, and those three words pretty much summed it up. Faith in "the good Lord" was all a person needed to get by. Even in the hard times.

Life was pretty nice in Red Cloud, for a while anyway. We had a garden, a few chickens, some pigs. Biscuits and gravy were usually on the table. Butter, too. Sometimes honey, if times were especially good. There was always a short prayer before we ate. Papa bowed his head with the rest of us, but the out-loud praying was left to Mama. She was pretty, my mom, and in good health most of her life. And she was always there for us, whenever we needed her.

We didn't have the nice things most other people did, but we were grateful for what we had. Hard as my parents worked, I never heard them complain. We never went to bed hungry, I remember that. When we were little, Mama would tuck us in bed with this prayer:

Now I lay me down to sleep, I pray the Lord my soul to keep.
If I should die before I wake, I pray the Lord my soul to take.
If I should live for other days, I pray the Lord to guide my ways.

Often she would tack on to the prayer something specific and personal, thanking the Lord for this or that, asking him to bless this person or that one. There was always something to be thankful for, but, as the Depression got worse, those things, like the honey on the table, became scarce.

From 1929 to 1932 personal income in Nebraska plummeted by almost 50 percent. My father's dropped even worse. Everyone in Red Cloud felt the pinch. Most were too poor to purchase shoes and clothes. You either bought glue-on soles or else put a piece of cardboard in your shoe to cover up the hole, replacing it weekly. Twenty-five-pound sacks of flour came with floral prints, which women used to make dresses. When the dresses became threadbare, the women kept wearing them, stitching up the hems, patching over the rips. Nobody had much, but they made do with the little they had.

Pop had to cobble together several part-time jobs to make ends meet. One of those was shucking corn for a farmer down the road. He walked two and a half miles to get there, then back again at the end of the day.

No one in Red Cloud had tractors or combines because no one could afford them, and so most everything, from haying to husking, was done by hand. I can still remember the process. You thumb-hooked the top of the husk, twisted it, gave it a good yank, then tossed the ear against the bangboard of a mule-drawn wagon. Bangboards were high wooden sides that kept the ears from spilling out. You knew it landed in the wagon when you heard the ear bang against the boards.

Corn had to be husked so it could dry in a crib without rotting. It was hard work, but it was honest labor. And steady—you could count on it every fall. The prices had been pretty stable, too: six cents a bushel. The workday started at sunup and ended at sundown. You could do 80 bushels a day—on a good day, 90. At six cents a bushel that's $5.40. Not bad for Red Cloud.

Just when you thought things in rural America couldn't get worse, the bottom fell out. Dust storms swept across the farms, or what was left of them. We put rags around the windows, under the doors, but still the dust found a way in, covering everything. Windblown dust collected in drifts around fences. Sand piled up against barns, against houses, against sheds. Dunes of sand, everywhere. With the heat, the drought, and the dust storms, the corn shriveled on the stalk.

Everything was in short supply, not just corn. Things like sugar, butter, gasoline, rubber, and tires were all rationed, which made it difficult if you had a family to support.

My parents had four mouths to feed besides their own, those belonging to three very hungry boys and a somewhat sickly girl. The six of us lived in a four-room house: two bedrooms, a kitchen with a wood-burning stove for cooking, and a living room with a potbelly stove for heating. My younger brothers and I slept in one of those bedrooms. My older sister shared my parents' room.

We all shared the outhouse . . . and a Sears catalog whose pages served as toilet paper.

Sears, Roebuck & Company. That catalog was my only window to the world outside Red Cloud, revealing how other people lived, what they owned, what they wore. *Did they really have so many things?* I wondered. *So many* nice *things?* Women's fashions were in the front of the catalog, but my mother's fingers passed over those pages, stopping on ones that advertised more practical things. A washing machine, for example, available with little money down and low monthly payments. An egg incubator would be nice. Or a hand cart to help in the garden.

I remember always looking forward to Christmas, and maybe that catalog had something to do with it, setting my mind to dreaming about things that wealthy families in big cities had. Even though we were poor, somehow my parents managed to get each of us a present—but only one. A pair of lace-up boots was an especially welcome gift for the long winter walks to and from school. A coat. A pair of overshoes for the snow. I remember receiving a pocketknife one year. That was quite a Christmas for a young boy.

We never owned a home, always leasing instead. The house I remember best was a small place with a barn. It had no electricity, no running water. Eventually, though, Pop drilled a well. My job was to pump it until the water filled a fifty-five-gallon drum.

Everyone in the family worked hard. Tending the garden. Carrying pails of water from the well to wherever it was needed—for the garden, for the dishes, for the weekly bath we took turns taking. Cooking. Canning. Raising chickens. Washing clothes in a machine you turned with a handle. Supper dishes. Mending clothes. Rendering lard. Making soap.

One of my jobs was to help my father down by the Republican River, where he cut down trees, crosscutting the wood so it could be used in stoves. I was at the other end of the saw, pulling as he pushed. We stopped only for lunch, which was usually a peanut butter and jelly sandwich, though sometimes, on a good day, it was ham. When we finished, we loaded the wood into our wagon, first stocking our own woodpile to see us through the winter, then we went door-to-door, selling off the rest.

He was a man of few words, my father. I guess his mind

was occupied with the job at hand—his example certainly taught me how to work hard. From him I learned how to take any circumstance, no matter how dire, and find the work in it. Take for example the Republican River Flood of 1935. It came rushing through Red Cloud one day with such fury that it tore up everything in its path. In total, almost a hundred lives were lost; in some towns, three-fourths of the homes were destroyed. It flooded our basement, but Pop made quick work of that so he could go on to paid labor. He took his team of horses and hauled things away, from uprooted trees to piles of debris that had stacked up on the county roads. The flood washed out the railroad tracks in town, but there was work to be found there, too, rebuilding them.

Both parents worked so long and hard there wasn't time or energy to read stories, which, as a kid, I would have loved. Perhaps it's just as well, as there was precious little light to read by at night. Most of the time the only illumination we had came from a kerosene lamp that sat on the table. By its warm circle of light, Mom darned clothes while Pop sharpened knives or did some other work to get ready for the next day.

Maybe that is why English was my favorite subject in school. I still remember my teacher, Mrs. Kellogg, taking us through *The Rime of the Ancient Mariner,* Coleridge's tale of an ill-fated sea voyage, narrated by the lone survivor.

Under the water it rumbled on,
Still louder and more dread,
It reach'd the ship, it split the bay;
The ship went down like lead.

Stunn'd by that loud and dreadful sound,
Which sky and ocean smote,
Like one that hath been seven days drown'd
My body lay afloat;
But swift as dreams, myself I found
Within the Pilot's boat.

As she read the poet's stanzas, the words lapped upon my young imagination. I had never seen the ocean, but it seemed to me a place of adventure, so different from the monotonous, midwestern plains of my youth. That there were darker, more complex themes—about loss, the guilt of survivors, and the mercy of God who loves "all things both great and small"—escaped me at the time. I would have to discover them for myself.

THERE HAD BEEN little hope things would turn around during the Herbert Hoover years, but when Franklin D. Roosevelt was sworn into office as president, the mood changed. On

March 4, 1933, FDR led his first inaugural address with the following words: "First of all, let me assert my firm belief that the only thing we have to fear . . . is fear itself." There was something in the way he spoke—the pauses he used, his calm, reassuring tone. There was a warmth in that voice, an understanding, an empathy. And the American people, especially those of us who had lost so much, were drawn to their radios to warm themselves by his words.

But the president's address did more than comfort us. It emboldened us—much the way a mariner might call to his fellow sailors in a storm, pointing them to safe harbor, calling to them over the howl of the wind, summoning them, all hands on deck, every oar manned, each back pulling against the waves. That's what his words did. They helped us locate our own strength. And finding it, we were filled with a resolve that the Depression had all but driven out of us.

Between 1929 and 1931, four thousand banks had collapsed. By 1933, that figure rose to nine thousand. The bank failures erased $2.5 billion in lost deposits, which, in turn, represented so many lost farms, lost homes, and vanished dreams. When FDR took office, one-fourth of the workforce sat idle. The Depression was not a respecter of class or creed. Bankers stood next to farmers in the same soup line. And when government programs offered jobs, they worked side by side, laying bricks to build a school or a post office.

Those programs, though, didn't find their way to Webster County. The ones that came arrived too late for people in the wasteland that was now southern Nebraska. Remember that woman from just outside Invale, who Timothy Egan related had started to burn her husband's diary? Well she didn't. Her neighbor's intervention saved it from the fire. Here are a few of the entries, which give a sense of what people in our parts went through.

April 5 [1938]
Verna has been doing a little sewing for different ones & I have been doing principally nothing. No income, only 2 horses left, 95 acres of mortgaged land, unpaid taxes & interest and $0 in cash. That's the outlook that faces us after I have lived more than 40 years in Nebr.

April 18
Well here it is Monday again & I haven't done a bit of farmwork yet & I don't know if I ever will. With only 2 horses, not a cent to our name, not a cent of income for the last 4 years I just don't know exactly where to turn.

July 24
Today is just common hell, death and destruction to every growing thing. A dry, deadly S. W. wind, a dead clear sky

& a viscious blazing sun make up the picture of destruction. God in his infinite wisdom might have made a more
discouraging place than Webster Co., Nebr., but so far as
I know God never did.

Those diary entries give a glimpse into what life was like
for those who made their living from the land, those in my
part of southern Nebraska any way. I suspect it wasn't much
different for folks in the panhandles of Texas and Oklahoma,
the plains of Kansas, the eastern parts of Colorado and New
Mexico. We needed something to hold onto, a hope of something on the horizon that was coming our way. An act of God,
intervening for us. A word from the good Lord, explaining
it all, helping us make sense of everything. Something. Anything. What came instead was a word from the president.

Eight days after his inauguration, Roosevelt broadcast his
first "fireside chat." He would hold thirty such radio addresses
over the course of his four terms. The president began his first
with the words, "My friends," as if to gather the country's
frightened families into his paternal arms. In simple language
that everyone could understand and with a reassuring voice
that anyone could trust, his appeals brought calm to the living
rooms of anxious American homes. He started his chat with
the words, "I want to talk for a few minutes with the people
of the United States about banking." And he ended it with
these: "It is your problem no less than it is mine. Together we

cannot fail." The president's we're-all-in-this-together way of framing the problem was so winsome that during the first one hundred days in office he received fifty thousand letters from people across the country who were moved to share their stories and express their thanks to him for renewing their hopes.

FDR wasn't all talk, of course. One of his most impactful initiatives was the Works Progress Administration (WPA), a sweeping infrastructure program that provided jobs for building schools, bridges, post offices, and other structures for the common good. He also increased defense spending to an unprecedented level.

Defense jobs were great opportunities, but they didn't come to Red Cloud. This suited me fine for the time being. My senior year stretched between 1939 and 1940, and the athletic teams I was involved in left little time for work outside the chores I had to do at home. I played four sports—football, basketball, track, and baseball. My senior year I was voted best all-around athlete, in a school of two hundred. Of all the sports, football was my favorite. I played center for a couple of years, then spent my last two years in the backfield. The team was small yet scrappy, though we never drew much of a crowd. High school football is nearly a religion in Nebraska these days, but people just didn't have the time back then. They worked from dawn through dusk, and by the time the sun went down, the games we played were over and done with.

When I wasn't playing sports or doing chores, I was working somewhere. In the summer I cut weeds in cornfields and worked on a threshing crew, pitching bundles of hay into the thresher. During the school year I scrubbed floors and stairways in some of the two-story buildings. Or delivered flyers from the Rexall drugstore and the small J. C. Penney in town.

My favorite job, though, was distributing ads for the cinema, mainly because the owner gave me free movie passes. The two-hundred-seat theater showed mostly westerns. Gene Autry. John Wayne. Tex Ritter. And of course, with every film came a newsreel. My father had served in the First World War, drafted into the infantry. He fought the Germans and was gassed while in combat, later developing heart problems because of it. He never spoke of the war he fought in—or of the one looming on the horizon. And so what I knew about the conflicts abroad, I learned from the newsreels in that theater.

Week by week they chronicled Hitler's march across Europe. One nation after another fell like so much wheat before the thresher. By the summer of 1940, France, Norway, Denmark, Belgium, Poland, and the Netherlands had joined Germany, Austria, and Czechoslovakia under Nazi domination. On the other side of the world, the Japanese had extended their reach into Korea, Manchuria, and Mainland China, grabbing more and more territory. People in my town watched those newsreels. They heard the president's speeches on their radios. They saw the covers of the *Life* magazines that had collected at the barbershop. They read the newspapers. Gradually the understanding took hold, at least in Red Cloud, that war was inevitable.

AFTER GRADUATING HIGH SCHOOL in May 1940, I didn't have much to look forward to. I thought about college, but that didn't pan out. I looked for full-time employment, but by now work in Red Cloud was hard to come by. I picked up some part-time jobs here and there during the summer, but they didn't pay well and there was no future in them.

It was during this time that a Navy recruiter came to town. He dressed in crisply pressed dark slacks and a jacket whose shoulders revealed his rank—chief petty officer. He set up a table and chairs in the post office, giving out literature to any young man who showed interest. He accurately pointed out to me that there was not much to do in Nebraska, but he said there was a veritable world of opportunity awaiting in the Navy. I listened to his pitch and took his literature. It didn't look so bad. They paid your way to see the world, giving you free room and board. And to top it off, a paycheck of twenty-one dollars a month. A *steady* paycheck.

A lot of boys joined the service for the same reason. Consider one of my future shipmates, John Evans, for example. He came from a family of six kids, and they all worked on the family's farm in the hills of Alabama. Later, when he was asked why he joined the Navy, his answer was, "I was hungry. My family was hungry, and that was a way to get food." He sent his money home, all of it. For spending cash, he shined the shoes of his shipmates, along with washing and pressing their clothes. His family, like mine and so many others, were the hardworking poor in America, struggling just to put food on the table. John joined the Navy not because of the impending threat of war, but because of the more immediate threat of his family's poverty. Countless others, myself included, signed up for the same reason. The Navy offered us a way out of that, and we took it.

I briefly weighed the decision against serving in the Army, as my father had, but when I thought about the long marches and crawling through the mud, cruising the high seas on the deck of a ship seemed the better alternative. I talked it over with my parents, and they felt if I wanted to enlist, it was my choice to make. I signed the paperwork in September 1940. I would leave in a month or so, I was told, bused to Omaha, then to Great Lakes, Illinois, for basic training.

During that time, Roosevelt ran for an unprecedented third term. His Republican opponent, Wendell Willkie, criticized him for not doing enough to build up the defenses of the country. After the November election, Roosevelt moved with an increased sense of urgency and pushed Congress to pass the Selective Training and Service Act, authorizing the first peacetime draft in American history.

Later that year, on December 29, 1940, FDR gave a fireside chat focusing on the "Arsenal of Democracy" that was American industry. When the war in Europe broke out in September 1939, our nation was officially neutral, but through the Lend-Lease Act, which Roosevelt signed into law in March 1941, we were able to supply armaments and ordnance for the democratic countries such as Great Britain that were at war with Germany and Japan. In *this* address, however, there was a shift in the president's message, informing the American people of the need to build up our own arsenal. The world, after all, was at war. And though the conflict had not come to our shores, the prudent thing to do was to store up something for our defense in case it did.

A surge of patriotic songs followed, as I remember. Supporting the draft was "He's A-1 in the Army, and He's A-1 in My Heart." The Andrews Sisters' tune "Boogie Woogie Bugle Boy" was nominated for an Academy Award for Best Song, having been featured in the Abbott and Costello movie *Buck Privates* (January 1941). "Arms for the Love of America" (May 1941), by Irving Berlin, buttressed the president's appeal to build up the country's arsenal. Then there was Mack Kay's "Goodbye Dear, I'll Be Back in a Year" (April 1941).

Most of us, though, would not be back in a year. Too many would never return at all. Of course, none of us knew it at the time.

In my case, they were preaching to the choir. I had al-

2

To Sea on the Arizona

It was to become the best-known musical band in the Pacific Fleet, assigned to what was to become the most famous ship in the world. . . . They were the musicians of Band No. 22, serving aboard the battleship Arizona *(BB-39).*

—Molly Kent,
USS Arizona's *Last Band*

In September 1940, I arrived for basic training at the Great Lakes Naval Training Center along Lake Michigan in northern Illinois. I took a bus to get there, a small bag of clothes in tow. Before I departed, I said my goodbyes to a few friends, none of whom had enlisted yet but who would later join me.

On the day I left home, my family saw me off. Life in the

Great Plains prepared a person for a lot of things, but not for goodbyes. Few people ever left the town they grew up in. Or even the land their parents worked. The same could be said for the church where they were baptized. People in our end of the Midwest didn't have thoughts of going off to New York or California to follow their dreams. And none of us would have ever thought of going off to see the world if some outsider hadn't come to town and put the idea into our heads.

I had no idea how my leaving home would affect my family. The bed my two brothers and I shared would be less crowded, and I'm sure they welcomed that. But the conversations we had before going to sleep and the laughter that sometimes punctuated those conversations, all that would change. They would have to divide my chores between them, shouldering more of the load. I could tell my leaving was hard on my sister, who had heart trouble and was in poor health her entire childhood, but she couldn't find words to say goodbye, either. And Pop, a reserved man on most occasions, had few words on that day. Perhaps he thought about his own military service, and about the terrible demands war might one day ask of his son. I would write, I promised Mama, knowing full well that words didn't come easy for me, either.

After hugs and a handshake and a mother's tears, I said goodbye to my family.

After I boarded the bus and settled into a seat, I looked through the back window and watched as Red Cloud grew smaller, until at last it was gone. I was saying goodbye to the life I had lived there, to virtually all the people I had known, to my whole identity. I didn't say it out loud, didn't even think it in words, didn't really want to consider this rending moment with my family that made my mama cry. It was just a vague, inarticulate feeling, somewhere deep. A knowing: I was leaving home for good.

It was a seven-hundred-mile bus ride across the farmlands of the central Midwest. Endless fields of corn passed by my window, their stalks standing tall in their fields, neat in their rows, awaiting harvest. Farmhouses interrupted the monotony of the landscape with weathered barns thirsting for paint and concrete-staved silos hungering for corn. The low, rolling hills had an almost hypnotic effect as they swelled and subsided, green with the beginnings of winter wheat. The broom-swept skies of sunset. The deep purple shadows of dusk. It was all so beautiful.

When I arrived at Great Lakes, there were lots of boys like me. Just as young. Equally naïve and eager to be setting off on a voyage to sail the globe as I was. Their skin was still a little pimply, like mine. And in their eyes was the same glint of adventure. There was an innocence about them, too, about me, and about the country we had all pledged to serve, the ink barely dry on the paperwork.

The hardest part of basic training, at least for me, was the routine. Reveille was at 5:30 A.M. Breakfast was at six, followed by a two-hour march we called a "grinder." Then rowing. Followed by rifle drills. Lunch. Afterward we sat in class for lectures from the officers. Swimming and lifesaving came after that in an indoor pool on the base. Then dinner.

Every day was just like the one before. For six long weeks. During all that time we never boarded a ship. We were taught *how* to board a ship, but we never actually got *on* one. We were also instructed on how to get ammunition from the ready box to the gun, but we never fired that gun. We were, however, taught how to get rid of the empty cartridges. It was called *"basic* training," I learned, for a reason.

When our training was over, the Navy sent us all home for a week, which was a nice break in the routine. In those six weeks, I saw more of the world than I had in the past eighteen years.

In mid-October 1940 I took a train west across neatly rowed farmland, vast empty plains, high desert, and mountain ranges to Bremerton, Washington, nestled in the misty evergreen forests of the Pacific Northwest. The train had originated back east, and there were a number of newly enlisted sailors from the eastern seaboard who had never seen the endless prairies of the Midwest, had never even seen a jackrabbit. They would gather around the windows, pointing when they saw one, remarking excitedly when they saw a bunch of them darting in all directions. It made the rest of us smile. I'm sure we midwesterners would have acted the same way if we passed New York City in a train, our faces pressed against the windows, pointing at the skyscrapers.

Once we spilled out of the train at Bremerton, I joined my shipmates and got the first look at my new home, the USS *Arizona* (BB-39). The sight of her stopped us. She was the biggest thing we had ever seen, and each of us stood in awe of her.

"Wow."

"Look at her, will ya."

"Take a look at those guns."

THE *ARIZONA* WAS 33,000 tons of tempered steel, bolted and welded together into a massive machine of war. Quite a sight for a flatlander like me. She, along with the USS *Pennsylvania,* were the two largest battleships in the Navy's fleet. At 608 feet, she was two football fields long. *Two.* And she was 97 feet wide, almost a third of a football field. She boasted four turrets, each featuring three .45-caliber, 14-inch guns that weighed 93 tons. And she had twenty-two .51-caliber, 5-inch antiaircraft guns and four .50-caliber, 3-inch guns. I never saw anything like it in my life. She was really something.

She had good bones, strong and sturdy. The keel of the ship had been laid on March 16, 1914. When completed, the ship was christened in the Brooklyn shipyards on June 19,

1915. The celebration was attended by seventy-five thousand people, including Franklin Roosevelt, then assistant secretary of the Navy under President Woodrow Wilson, who also was there for the ceremony. She was later commissioned into the Navy in 1916 for service in World War I. Ironically, she stayed stateside for the war's duration. She had never seen action before I arrived.

That flush of awe quickly left me the first time I stepped aboard. She had been drydocked, and her deck was congested with shipyard workers—welders with their blowtorches spewing sparks, electricians splicing cords that occasionally popped, carpenters replacing some of the planks in the deck. Woven through all this was a tangle of cables, ropes, and hoses.

The chaos on board was overwhelming to a kid from the middle of nowhere. I remember anxiously thinking, *Oh, boy, this isn't really what I anticipated.* As I stood there, one of the chaplains (the ship had three: Protestant, Catholic, and Jewish), a Lutheran named Thomas Kirkpatrick, walked by and stopped to talk. He must have sensed I was unsettled. "This isn't always the way it is, my friend. Everything will get better," he said calmly, "once we go to sea."

Like a big gray beached whale, she seemed so out of place in the Puget Sound Navy Yard. We were immediately put to work scraping barnacles off her hull and slathering on paint. The fumes often got so strong that you would get "paint-drunk" before the day was out. The work went on nonstop, twenty-four hours a day, and we all helped shoulder it. I helped mostly with the chipping and painting, and that is where I learned to appreciate how well built she was.

She had several decks, the most impressive being the main deck, which was made of teak. Though it is an exceptionally hard wood, teak had to be continually maintained by a process called holystoning. The original holystones came from pieces of stone cut from medieval churches, which is how they got their name; in time, bricks replaced stones. We would wet the deck, put a fine dusting of sand and lime over it, then take a brick with a hole in it and push it over the planks with a pole. Afterward we washed away the sand and lime and mopped the deck until it shined. We did this eight to ten times per plank until the deck looked like new. The ritual was repeated, religiously, once a week.

We were in Bremerton about three months, then sailed down the Pacific Coast to sunny Long Beach, California. Finally, in April 1940, she was sent 2,500 miles across the ocean to the palm-treed paradise of Hawaii.

Sure enough, as the chaplain said, once we went to sea, everything *did* get better.

THE *ARIZONA* HOUSED 1,512 officers, sailors, and Marines, a population about the size of Red Cloud. The small town that was the *Arizona* held everything we had back home—a general store, a barber shop, soda fountain, post office, print shop, newspaper, dentist office, sick bay, and a brig.

There was no way to meet everyone on board, but you did get to know the men in your division. The ship was sectioned off into seven divisions, each comprising fifty to sixty men. I was placed in the sixth. A lot of the sailors in my division had been in the Navy for some time and had photo albums of the places in the world where the Navy had taken them. They were quick to share them, along with the stories that went with them—and I was an eager audience.

Each man slept either in a hammock or on a cot. I got the hammock, which was made of stiff, white canvas. It was tight quarters with three tiers of hammocks, and you had to give the cinch a good pull so you wouldn't sag down on the sailor below you. Also, if you slept with a sag in your hammock, you woke up with a backache. To keep the hammock from enfolding around you like a cocoon, you had to insert spreaders—1x1x16-inch wooden sticks with notches on either end—in the two outside ropes at each end.

The daily routine almost never varied. Reveille was at 5:30 A.M., breakfast at six. Meals were served in the same compartment we slept in. The first thing we did after getting up was to stow the hammocks and cots in the bins along the outside bulkhead. That cleared space so the mess cooks could come and set up the tables and benches that were stowed in the overhead compartments. Once the white porcelain dishes and the stainless-steel flatware were laid out, they brought the food, served family-style. Meals were always good, even on the days when we had beans. We were served beans on Wednesday and Saturday mornings. Not ham and beans. Not some other main dish and beans. Beans. With ketchup on the side. And a square of corn bread. "Navy beans" were perfect for long voyages, because they were nutritious, low in cost, and could be stored for long periods of time.

The behavior around the table was always mannerly. The senior-rated man at each table was responsible for the conduct. Only after the food had been passed around and everyone had taken a serving could you ask for seconds. The tables were left out during the day, then broken down and stowed after dinner.

Gradually I got more acquainted with the ship. She had six boiler rooms with four direct-drive steam engines that propelled her through the water at a speed of 21 knots. When fully loaded, though, she could only do 12. She had a steering compartment that required sixteen men to manually turn four large steering wheels in case the automatic steering ever failed to function. Fortunately, it never did, but the men were always there and ready. From wrestling with those wheels, the men had tremendous upper-body strength.

It took five uneventful days to get to Hawaii. I didn't even get seasick, though I think that had less to do with my constitution and more to do with the ship's construction. A battleship takes the undulations of the sea better than, say, a destroyer or a smaller vessel.

The crew was steady, too. There was a lot of respect between the men, regardless of whether you were an officer or an enlisted man. And there was plenty of trust—you never had to worry about anybody stealing anything. There was a clear code of conduct, and we lived by it. It was not much different from life back home, where there was a clear line between parents and kids, and heaven help you if you stepped across that line or forgot your manners or behaved at the supper table like a hog at a trough.

WHEN WE SAILED into Pearl Harbor, nestled in the south coast of the Hawaiian island of Oahu, tugboats met us, and a pilot boarded the ship to guide her safely to her berth.

How do I describe what Hawaii was like before the developers, putting up high-rises and housing developments; before the marketers, hawking timeshares; before the cruise ships, bursting at the seams with tourists; before the airlines, bringing in people from the four corners of the world, not to mention hordes of honeymooners?

The territory of Hawaii (it would not become a state until 1959) was paradise, a Shangri-la in the South Pacific, unspoiled by the rest of the world. The climate was invigorating; the air, clean and pure. The beaches were sandy, fringed with palms that caught the passing breeze in their fronds. In the moonlight, you would have sworn they were dancing. The surf washing against the shores was so peaceful it lulled you to sleep. The moon cast its silver glow across the harbor. *Magical.* No other word could describe it.

Showers were gentle, lasting only a part of an afternoon, rinsing everything. When the sun would come out, the most striking of rainbows would appear, each color vivid and distinct. The smell after one of those showers, I'll never forget it. The air, so clean you could almost distinguish the scents of individual flowers. Hibiscus. Lavender. Oleander.

Flowers were everywhere, lining streets, pouring down walls, spilling over fences. Orchids, which we view as rare here, were common over there. And the bougainvillea, rosy and purplish, bursts of color, cascading over roofs. It was like . . . well . . . it was how you imagined heaven would look, or hoped it would, anyway.

Outside the city of Honolulu were cane fields and pineapple plantations, bordered by low, rolling mountains and long stretches of deserted beaches. It was advertised as "A World of Happiness in an Ocean of Peace." And indeed it was, to my eye.

There was no smog, no snarls of traffic clogging up intersections. There weren't even traffic lights. They had good-natured traffic directors who stood at intersections, waving you by or signaling for you to stop. They often wore leis as they sat on their stools, watching as the tide of people floated by them on another uneventful day on the beat.

Of course there was poverty and injustice in Hawaii just as there was in every other corner of human society, but in my experience the people of Oahu were exceptionally friendly and hospitable, free from the time-is-money nonsense that is so pervasive in our "mainland" culture. Trolleys crisscrossed Honolulu at a slow pace. As a rule, the bars were not rowdy and raucous. Of course, there were exceptions, but mostly they were decent establishments, clean places, with piano music streaming out the front door or maybe the strum of a banjo or ukulele.

Shore leave, when you could get it, was whatever you wanted it to be. It could mean a day at Waikiki Beach, swimming, surfing, or just reading a good book in the shade. Or it might become a day of sightseeing in Honolulu, taking in the museum there, or the aquarium. If we were feeling more adventurous, there were jeep rides around the island, or perhaps a hike up Diamond Head, the volcano that dominates the Honolulu skyline. At night there was a steak dinner at a nice restaurant (cattle ranches were well established on the islands), taking in a picture show, drinks at a bar with a few of your buddies. Big bands performed at the Royal Hawaiian Hotel, which hosted a lot of dances and was a popular hot spot.

Then there was Honolulu's notorious Hotel Street, where

lines of soldiers and sailors waited for their turn with the women who worked there. On shore leave, sailors had to wear their uniforms, and on a Friday or Saturday night, Hotel Street looked like a slow-moving river of white.

If you didn't get shore leave, though, life aboard ship was still pretty good, not something you felt desperate to get away from. On the fantail, which is the deck nearest the stern, movies were shown. A special projection booth was mounted alongside the No. 3 turret on the port side, and a screen was set up on the stern. Officers sat in chairs, enlisted men stood. The movies were fairly current, and we all loved them. They had church services on the fantail, too. They weren't mandatory, but a lot of fellas went. Although I was then, and still am now, fairly reserved about my faith, I did carry a small New Testament in my shirt pocket. It was a good reminder, having it so close to my heart, of all that my mama modeled to me in my growing-up years. Sometimes a person forgets things like that, especially being an ocean away from what you know is the right way to live a life.

Sports built a lot of camaraderie among the men. Each ship had a team of some kind—football, boxing, wrestling, rowing. Being an athlete in high school, I jumped at the opportunity, signing up for the football and rowing teams. Boxing, though, was the favorite sport of most men. Challenges were made between individual ships, and spirited matches were fought on their decks.

That's where I first heard of Joe George, a boxer from the *Vestal,* a repair ship that maintained the fleet. Joe had quite a reputation for his fights inside the ring—three times All-Navy and once international Golden Gloves champion. He also had earned a reputation for his fights *outside* the ring—a number of courts-martial and an even greater number of days in the brig. The Navy's term for shore leave is "liberty," and some of the men, like George, took the term literally. I can't speak for the sailors on other ships, but most of the time our ship-mates were well behaved when they were given liberty. There *was* trouble to be found, though, if you went looking for it. Invariably alcohol would lubricate the path. Those who did find trouble might also awake to discover themselves in the brig the next morning, nursing a headache, regretting the black mark that was put on their record and the stiff fine that went with it. This happened to George quite a bit, from what I heard. He was an ox of a man from Georgia, and when he got to drinking, inevitably a fight would break out, and he usually would be in the middle of it. He and his superior officer, Captain Cassin Young, often got crossways with each other about the liberties George took while ashore.

OF ALL THE opportunities for entertainment aboard the *Arizona,* nothing compared to the ship's band, which consisted of twenty-one men. The bandleader was the oldest member, at thirty-one; the youngest was seventeen. The rest ranged from the late teens to early twenties—just boys, really. They sported nicknames like Killer, Brick, Buttercup. Each name had a story behind it, often funny, sometimes embarrassing. Buttercup, for example, got his name from getting severely seasick the moment the ship set out for open waters.

The band members had come from all over the country, from Pasadena, Texas, to the East Meadow of Long Island, New York. Some had attended prestigious music conservatories, like Juilliard. Others had graduated from piddly schools, like Okmulgee High, in Oklahoma. Before they joined the Navy, the boys in the band worked a variety of jobs. One was a movie usher. Another, a soda jerk. Still another, a ranch hand. One was a state champion wrestler. Another was a baton twirling teacher.

The one thing that brought them together and bonded them together was the music. They had all met at the U.S. Navy School of Music in Washington, D.C., and on May 23, 1941, had graduated together, and so before they were ever assigned to a ship, they were a tight-knit group. Once assigned to the *Arizona,* they were designated as Band Unit No. 22. Not the most catchy name for a band, but they soon made a name for themselves.

On July 17, Band Unit No. 22 came on board BB-39. They arrived with their instruments, bringing with them a mixed bag of big-band music, jitterbug, jazz, and swing. Our previous band had been made up of older musicians who played mostly older music. This young band sounded more like the groups led by Benny Goodman, Glenn Miller, or the Dorsey Brothers, playing favorites like "Chattanooga Choo-Choo," "String of Pearls," and "You Made Me Love You."

Back when we were stationed in Bremerton, we were ordered to give up our radios and put them in storage. I didn't own one myself, but I liked listening to the music from some of my buddies' radios. *Now* we had something even better. Now we had our own band, our own music. And were they ever something.

The first time we heard them play, we couldn't believe our luck in having them on *our* ship. They played for morning colors, gave concerts before movies, played at church services, too. Services were held Sunday morning on the quarterdeck in the open air, the tables and benches covered by a large square of canvas to shade us from the sun. It almost looked like a revival tent. And the music, well, it wasn't anything like I heard at the Methodist church in Red Cloud.

The band was amazingly adaptable. They could be a jazz ensemble one night, an orchestra the next, an up-tempo dance group on still another evening. Soon they were in demand, playing at events as diverse as boxing matches and birthday parties. There were seventeen Navy bands at Pearl Harbor, stationed either on ships or onshore, along with one Marine band. The groups were competitive, which led someone to come up with the idea of having a "Battle of Music," letting audiences decide which band was best. The ongoing contest continued through the fall and was scheduled to end on December 20, when the finals were to be held.

On every other Saturday night, beginning on September 13, 1941, four bands competed against each other, and the top two would advance to the next round in the competition. Winners were determined by the applause of the audience. On the first night of the competition, which was held at Bloch Arena, the four bands were from the *California, West Virginia, Dobbin,* and *Arizona.* We took first place; the *California* took second. First- and second-place winners advanced to the next stage of competition. Our band advanced to the first semifinal, which was held November 22. The Marine Corps Barracks band, which had the most men in the audience, cheering them, took first place. Our band came in second and qualified for the final four. The second semifinal round was to be held December 6 to determine the remaining two groups that would vie for the championship on December 20.

EVEN THOUGH THEIR rehearsals and their performances took up most of their time, the band worked elbow to elbow with the rest of us. Our days were filled with drills. When we weren't drilling, we were painting. And when we finished painting, there was more drilling. The cycle was endless.

During the course of 1941, the fleet got painted three times. The *entire* fleet! When we were in the Navy Yard at Bremerton, we painted our ship what they called "Navy gray." In the spring we painted her black above the waterline and red below it. Then someone high up got the idea to paint gray and black zigzag patterns on the ships as a kind of camouflage, called "dazzle." The logic wasn't ever explained to us enlisted men. We didn't rub shoulders with the officers; there were dividing lines between the two that you didn't cross. One of those lines was that you never questioned an order. You just did what you were told. And so if you were ordered to paint zigzags, you did zigzags. If you were told polka dots, you painted polka dots. There was a clear chain of command, and enlisted men were the last link of that chain. Apparently someone higher up in the chain of command didn't like the zigs or maybe it was the zags, because the next order was to paint the ships various shades of blue, from light to navy.

After the painting stopped, the drills started. Each week the ships went on maneuvers a couple of hundred miles away from the harbor, usually going out to sea on a Monday and returning on a Friday.

On maneuvers, designated ships would pull dummy targets ten, fifteen, sometimes twenty miles out from where our ships were. The targets were the size of a five-room house, and we could hit the target three out of five times from twenty miles away. To give perspective, a man with an unaided eye can see roughly only twelve miles when at sea, to where the horizon disappears. The shell goes eight miles *past* that. They weighed anywhere from 1,800 to 2,500 pounds; they were so big you could see them flying through the air. The purpose of these big guns was to pound a site. To hit it again and again and again until it was pummeled. It could be a beachhead, or a fortress in the hills overlooking that beach.

Each of us had been assigned a battle station. Even the boys in the band had one. I came across a letter written by one of those sailors to his sister, and I will let him tell you in his own words about their responsibilities aboard ship. His name was Clyde Williams. His sister, who later wrote a book about the band, was Molly.

Here's what we do on a battleship. We get up at 5:30 A.M.
and eat at six-thirty. At seven-thirty, we go down below to
the third deck and warm up until 7:45. At 8 o'clock, we play
colors. (That's when the flag goes up on the stern-post.) We go
in and those not in the dance band clean up the compartment.

At nine-thirty, we start rehearsal. Sometimes it is dance
band and sometimes concert band. We play until eleven, and
then eat our noon meal. At twelve-thirty, we play a noon con-
cert and then go back to rehearse until four.

Next comes chow. At five-thirty, we give a dance band
concert until six-thirty.

*After all, we are free to do anything we want to do, unless
there's a drill.*

*Sundays we play for church and get off in the afternoon
sometimes.*

*In case of fire or collision, we fall in at the sick bay as
stretcher bearers. In case of an attack by air or sea, we fall in
down on the third deck at the ammunition hoists to send ammunition to the guns topside. When we go into actual battle,
our horns will be left ashore and we will be detailed to the
sick bay to take care of the wounded, pick up stray arms and
legs, etc.*

My own battle station was the port antiaircraft director
on the sky-control platform. In short, our job was to operate
the *Arizona*'s five port-side antiaircraft guns. The director
unit hung on the ship's mast, one deck above the bridge, and
we had to scale several flights of steel ladders to get to it. It
was a cubical structure, made of steel. Ten men were assigned
to each director (our ship had two: one on the starboard side,
the other on the port). Inside the cubicle, the director itself
sat on a track with cogs, and you could hear them clicking
as you turned the dials. We practiced twice a week, and we
got to the point where we were synchronized with each other
as smoothly as the gears in a fine watch. From the director
we could fix the .25-caliber antiaircraft guns on any incoming planes. Our gunnery officer, Ensign Frank Lomax, would

rattle off a shorthand of staccato instructions: "Screen forward, aft. Distance, three thousand yards." And we would synchronize the dial and range finder, send the signal to one of the guns, then set it on automatic, and the guns would fire, based on the coordinates we had fed into the director.

Besides being posted to battle stations, each of us was assigned to some other job. Mine was the incinerator, a rectangular room with a big furnace and a venting pipe going up the smokestack. My partner, Harl Nelson, and I were responsible for feeding discarded boxes, both wooden and cardboard, into the furnace, along with all the burnable trash. We were the only two on that job, so if something was to be burned, we were the ones who burned it. We worked together for about six months. It was good to have a buddy with you, because it was pretty boring work. We also went on shore leave together, where we might go to the north end of the island to watch the pipeline waves that Hawaii was so famous for, or to the south end of the island to watch the geyser spew. Those may seem pretty tame entertainment for a couple of sailors on leave, but Harl was from Arkansas and I was from Nebraska, and, well, you just don't see things like waves and geysers in our neck of the woods.

THE *ARIZONA* WAS scheduled to return to Bremerton, Washington, in late November for an overhaul in their shipyard.

We were all looking forward to it. It meant we would get to spend December in the States, celebrate Christmas there, maybe even be given leave to go home.

In October, though, those plans abruptly changed. We were on maneuvers from October 18 to 26, and the weather was foggy and rainy almost the entire time. The schedule had been stepped up during that month. None of the officers told us why. We wondered what they knew that we didn't. Of course, we didn't ask. They added zigzag maneuvers—timed turns made in unison with other ships—to the normal routine of target practice. They were evasive moves to be used if submarines were in the area or whenever she was in range of an enemy's big guns.

The officer of the deck coordinated the turns. He would set us all on a certain course, then, after several minutes, he would signal to change direction. Our lookouts were on the bridge and in the crow's nest, watching to make sure we were in sync with the other ships. But on October 22, visibility during those maneuvers was poor. A lot of fog. Compounding the problem, none of our ships had radar, and so we couldn't tell where we were in relation to the other ships.

"We were doing maneuvers," explained Clint Westbrook, who was belowdecks at the time, "changing column, line-of-bearing maneuver, and we were in the third step of the maneuver, when everybody looked out to the port side and there's the [Oklahoma] bearing down on us. I think the collision alarm went off. You manned pretty much the same station you would at general quarters. So everybody was in the process of dashing madly to their post when it hit, 'cause I went off the ladder and it knocked me right off."

Jim Lawson had just stepped out of the shower when he felt the collision. "There was a smack and I'm sitting on my behind in that washroom. I thought we'd been hit by a torpedo, so I wasted no time getting out of there, and topside I went. I got to my gun station just in time to see the other battleship rounding the fantail.

"Fortunately they had somehow got wind of the fact that they were on a collision course with the *Arizona* and they were on full astern when they hit us. But they went scraping along the side—you can imagine what that sounded like."

"We thought we were going to sink," recalled my shipmate Jim Foster. "It pitched and rolled. We finally took on water on the other side to get it right."

What happened was that all the battleships had been following with precision the directions the officer on deck had given. Each was sailing in a straight line, then, on his command they made a sharp starboard turn. Somehow the *Oklahoma* fell out of sync with the rest of us, causing the accident. I was asleep in my hammock at the time, roughly between ten and eleven at night, and the collision jolted me awake. It scraped off the port-side blisters—honeycombed metal buffers that had been installed on the outer hull to absorb a hit from a torpedo—and tore a hole in the hull big enough to drive a hay truck through.

The major consequence of the mishaps was that we had to spend time in drydock to get patched up, delaying our trip to Bremerton. And so instead of sailing for the West Coast in late November 1941 as scheduled, we would be remaining at Pearl Harbor through December. There's no moping in the Navy, but the collision certainly put a dent in morale when we got the news, since we were all looking forward to being stateside for Christmas.

There were other, graver, reasons to be concerned as well.

NOT MUCH INFORMATION filtered down from the officers, but their mood had shifted. We all felt it. They seemed more serious, more intense. Before October, there had been only occasional sightings of Japanese submarines. Lately, there had been not only more sightings but closer ones, too, just off the Hawaiian coast. The pace picked up. There were more drills, and they were longer and more intense. There was no idle chatter, no joking around. This was serious.

We got out of drydock on November 12 and went to sea again. This time we stayed out longer than normal, around two weeks, as I recall. We were on high alert, because there had been numerous sonar blips indicating the presence of submarines. Though we fired in their direction from time to time, we never hit one. Mostly they ran silent and deep, but they were running shallower now, at periscope depth, apparently not to attack but merely to observe. They were charting our movements, we surmised, trying to detect patterns in our movement, looking for any points of vulnerability.

But why? We weren't at war.

All I know is, we all felt better when we returned to the harbor. But we didn't stay long. In late November, we left port again, and weren't scheduled to return until December 5. Maneuvers usually beat painting, but we all felt uneasy about *this* maneuver. The fleet anchored on Lahaina Roads, which was an old fishing village on the west end of Maui. There wasn't much to do on the island, but it was a great place for R&R. A number of the men were given the afternoon off for shore leave. By midnight, they all returned refreshed and hit the sack.

But shortly after they had gone to bed, around 1:00 A.M., the general alarm went off, startling us out of our hammocks and sending us to our battle stations. Our destroyers and submarines that were on watch that night detected a number of sonar readings that could only be Japanese subs. Every sailor manned his station, every lookout scoured the sea. Though we weren't at war, it was starting to feel that way. The entire fleet, at Admiral Isaac C. Kidd's order, weighed anchor and put out to sea. There was no rest that night, for any of us. Sensing the subs were not a threat, the admiral had us sail for open seas and conduct gunnery maneuvers, as planned.

The day before we returned to Pearl, football practice had been scheduled. It would be a great way to relieve the tension everyone was experiencing. We had a big game scheduled for next Sunday, Navy versus Army, and the entire island was looking forward to it. It was now Thursday before game day, and we had a lot of work to do as a team. Right there on the deck, with the sea our only stadium, the sun our only audience, we practiced our plays. Running, passing, tackling, loving every minute of it. It was a great reprieve from thinking about the possibility of war.

Then an officer came up to us.

We stood at attention, saluting him. He told us practice was canceled. We groaned, looking at him in dismay. He then said Sunday's game was also canceled. The groans gave way to "whys," which he ignored. He continued, telling us that not only was this Sunday's game canceled, but the entire season was over. He ordered us to put our gear away and turn it in to the athletic locker when we reached port.

We were disappointed, of course, but we also grasped there was a reason for what he did. He knew something we didn't.

It must be war.

What other explanation could the Navy have for canceling the entire season?

3

The Last Night

The fleet sailed into harbor on Friday, December 5, and tugboats helped position the ships so they could tie up to their
respective quays, which were concrete structures built in the
water close to shore, to which ships fastened their mooring

lines. It took the better part of the day to get all the ships moored.

It felt great being back in the harbor. One of the reasons was that when we were out to sea, fresh water was rationed. Each day we were given a three-gallon bucket of water, which was all the ship's evaporator could produce. With those three gallons we had to bathe, shave, and wash our clothes. When we returned to harbor, though, we could take *real* showers. And, if you got up early enough, you could take a hot one. Hot water was always in short supply, at least for us enlisted men.

My friend Harl Nelson and I had been cleared for liberty, and we both went ashore that night to stretch out our land legs and take in the sights of the city. For some reason, though, Harl didn't seem his old self. As the night wore on, he grew more and more tired. I noticed a yellowing in his eyes and in his skin, and I talked him into going back to the ship and checking himself into sick bay.

Joe George, so I heard, had liberty that Friday night as well and was slated to fight in a "smoker." Smokers were boxing matches held at the recreation center in Honolulu. If you won, you wouldn't get money, which was against Navy rules, but you could receive a gift of some sort, such as a watch. You would then turn around and sell the watch, often to the very person who gave it to you. George did that a lot.

After the smoker, he celebrated his win by getting drunk,

which led to a fight with one of his own shipmates. Well, Shore Patrol came and broke up the fight, then took George to the ship's brig. The next morning he was escorted to the captain's mast to face Captain Young. The captain was so angry to see George disgrace his ship again and bring dishonor to his shipmates, he lashed out at him. "I wish I could take you to the forecastle and have all hands kick the shit out of you. But since I can't, I'm going to give you a summary court-martial."

Joe was immediately put on report and sentenced to become a prisoner at large—PAL, for short—which meant he didn't have to do time in the brig; he only had to be watched and restricted by the ship's master-of-arms, who happened to be a friend. And so, on the night of December 6, instead of being locked belowdecks in the brig, he spent it sleeping under the stars in the forecastle.

The next morning the *Arizona* took on a full load of fuel oil, nearly 1.5 million gallons, in preparation for her upcoming trip to Bremerton. The trade winds blew steadily over the island that morning, but the heavy smell of oil still lingered. Besides that, the ship held 180,000 gallons of aviation fuel for the scouting planes it had on board and over a million pounds of gunpowder in the forward magazines for the big guns. There was enough fuel on board to get us to Japan, and nearly enough firepower to sink the entire Imperial Fleet, should Hirohito be foolhardy enough to fire so much as a round across our bow.

The *Arizona* moored on the shore side of Ford Island. The repair ship *Vestal* sidled up next to our seaward side and she moored there. On board the *Vestal* was a welder's shop, pipe and copper shop, carpenter's shop, shipfitter's shop, boiler shop, blacksmith's shop, machine shop, electrical shop, and gyro repair shop. The men on that ship were old salts, many of them, and they had been around so long they had fixed most everything on the Pacific Fleet at one time or another. On Monday, they would be rebricking the *Arizona*'s boilers, repairing her generators, and putting new countertops in the kitchen.

By Saturday afternoon the wind had died down, the sun was warm, and the sky was clear, with the exception of a few cumulus clouds that had gathered to watch a civilian football game. The University of Honolulu stadium brimmed with twenty-five thousand hometown fans cheering their Silverswords in their game against the Willamette Bearcats from Oregon.

No one in the stadium seemed bothered by the rumors that a major Japanese offensive might be in the works. In fact, no one on the island seemed bothered, and that included those of us moored in the harbor. There were, however, concerns: whispers that a Japanese amphibious force would land on the other side of the island and mount an attack; rumors that Japanese expatriates living in Hawaii would conspire to sabotage some of the planes, maybe even some of the ships.

Of all the possibilities, though, no one was imagining something as bold and brazen as an all-out attack by air. The island was simply too far away from Japan, it was argued, to pull off such an attack without being detected first. Besides, we thought, the Japanese were poorly equipped, poorly trained, and, it was added almost with a smirk, no match for *our* men and *our* firepower.

Journalists were among those who thought that way. Clarke Beach, for example, in a September 6 article for the local newspaper, the *Star-Bulletin*, wrote, "A Japanese attack on Hawaii is regarded as the most unlikely thing in the world, with one chance in a million of being successful."

Enlisted men also were some of the ones who thought that way. Men like Clyde Nelson, one of the band members. He wrote home on November 20:

After being in the Navy for a year away from home and a lot of time under war conditions, I can see how much Pate [father] and the rest of the American legion can celebrate the day their war ended. It will be a great day when these war scares are over.

I find that the guys in the Navy don't think that we will ever engage in a fighting war. If we do, though, you can feel safe because there isn't a Navy afloat that can get by ours. I know because I've watched them fire and they don't miss.

Officers in Hawaii thought that way, too. At a staff meeting on November 26, Admiral Husband E. Kimmel asked Charles McMorris, his fleet officer in charge of wartime strategy, what he thought about the possibility of a Japanese air attack. The captain responded confidently, "None, absolutely none!"

That kind of thinking went as high as the secretary of the Navy, Frank Knox. Speaking to a private gathering in Washington on the evening of December 4, he announced: "I want you to know that whatever happens, the United States Navy is ready! Every man at his post, every ship at its station. . . . Whatever happens, the Navy is not going to be caught napping."

ON DECEMBER 6, 1941, our naval base was put on Alert No. 1, a warning to watch for small acts of sabotage, here and there. For this reason the airplanes were bunched together. And the ships, too, were arranged in tight rows. The consensus was that if you bunched everything close together, they would be easier to defend.

In spite of the low level of alert, there were those with premonitions of a greater attack. On a highway overlooking the harbor, the wife of Captain James W. Chapman took in the panoramic view and said, "If the Japanese are going to attack Hawaii, this would be the ideal time, for there sits the entire Pacific Fleet at anchor."

Later in the evening, Lieutenant Commander Edwin Layton was in the ballroom of the Royal Hawaiian Hotel with other officers, enjoying the night's festivities, when the band played "The Star-Spangled Banner." As everyone sang along, he later recounted that he had a terrible urge to jump up and shout, "Wake up, America!"

"On December 6, no one on Oahu was more overconfident than the military," writes historian Thurston Clarke, summarizing the attitude on the eve of December 7. Clarke quotes Richard Sutton, a young ensign attached to Admiral Claude Bloch: "We had the supreme overconfidence a great athlete has who has never been beaten—we all thought we were invincible."

SINCE THE BATTLESHIPS had to be fully manned at all times, only a fraction of my shipmates got shore leave the evening of December 6. All the members of the band got to go ashore, though, because the second round of semifinals for the Battle of Music was being held at Bloch Arena at the Pearl Harbor Naval Station. But they didn't go to play. They went to eye their competition and to catch up with some of the band members from the *Tennessee,* who were good friends from their days at music school.

I have a photograph of them, taken in November. It looks like a picture you would see in a high school yearbook, the boys having just been told by the photographer to sit up straight, look at the camera. Spread upon their music stands was their sheet music. Across their legs was a saxophone, a cornet, or some other instrument they had trained on for the greater part of their young lives. With a click, their innocence was captured in a glossy, black-and-white photograph, and suspended in time.

They were so good, you can't imagine. They must have been full of dreams of going professional after their hitch in the Navy was up. Maybe they would play in a big band, like the one Glenn Miller had, or Benny Goodman. Or perhaps some of them would start their own group. Maybe all of them together would start one. Who knows? When you're young and you have that kind of music running through you, there's no limit to where your dreams could take you.

By now, the islanders had caught on to how exceptional the *Arizona*'s band was. Even individual members were noted. Curt Haas played the sweetest flute you ever heard, it was said. Charles White was singled out as outstanding on the snare drum. And Bill Moorhouse, everyone remarked, played the best cornet they had ever heard.

Curt also played the clarinet and saxophone. He sang, too. Even wrote some of the arrangements. He was a quiet kid from the town of North Kansas, Missouri. His family called him "Buster."

Charles not only played the snare drum, he played the piano. On the side, he was learning to play several other instruments. He was a happy kid, with an outgoing personality. He was nicknamed "Whitey."

And Bill, he was one of the more athletic ones in the band. He swam, played golf. And did both with distinction, or so I was told.

The man responsible for honing all this young talent?

Fred Kinney. Fred had been in school with them all at the U.S. School of Music, and he handpicked each one of them. He worked with them individually, in small groups, and all together, pouring himself into every one of them. His goal? Making them the best band to graduate that year. And they were. By now they were even better—many thought they were the finest in the fleet.

For those left aboard ship that night, there were plenty of activities to keep us busy. On the fantail, they were showing the Spencer Tracy movie, *Dr. Jekyll and Mr. Hyde*. There was also a special ceremony where Admiral Kidd would be giving commendations for outstanding achievement to many of the athletes for their respective sports.

A little over a hundred of our men got liberty that night. Before they were allowed to leave, though, they had to be inspected by the officer of the deck. Uniforms had to be cleaned and pressed, shoes shined. After inspection, the officer's assistant handed out liberty cards. They gave a final salute, asked for permission to leave the ship, then boarded buses to

Honolulu. Curfew varied by rank, most of the men returning at midnight. If you were a petty officer, though, curfew was 2 A.M. Only married men who were living ashore and a few select officers were allowed to spend the night.

Many of the men would go to the Royal Hawaiian Hotel, because the big bands played there, doing concerts and dances. Others would visit their favorite restaurants, then take in a first-run film at one of the theaters. There were ample bars in Honolulu, and some of the men would go there, too. Plenty of tattoo parlors, as well. The one often led to the other. I visited the parlors a few times myself, coming out with two birds, a ship, and my initials. And, of course, some men took their place in line on Hotel Street.

I spent the night on deck. I had a cot stowed in the incinerator room for whenever I wanted to escape the heat, the snoring, and the cramped quarters belowdecks in our casemate. I set it up on the overhang of the superstructure where the Sixth Division was. I slept out there pretty regularly. I could hear the water break against the shore, and it soothed me.

The ship had "lights out" at 10 P.M., and, since most of the men were still ashore, it was quiet. The night was clear and balmy, a soft breeze blowing across the deck, sweeping the smell of fuel out to sea. I could hear a tropical bird on Ford Island, its song as familiar to me now as the voice of an old friend. For a long time I just lay there, looking up at the stars shimmering in the night sky. The moon was almost full, and it hung there like a cameo. It was all peaceful, so serene, and I felt my thoughts melting away.

As I lay there, I didn't think about the collision with the *Oklahoma*. It never even crossed my mind. But now, looking back, I realize how pivotal that accident had been in my life, in so many of our fates. Had it not happened, the *Arizona* would have been docked in the Pacific Northwest, and I would have been preparing to go home to Red Cloud for Christmas. Cold as it got in Nebraska, with just a potbellied stove to keep us warm, I missed home. Missed the wind as it blew through our house, finding cracks in the walls and filling the house with its shrill music. I missed the creativity of my mama, stitching together Christmas from the meagerest of threads and some-how coming up with a patchwork of memories for her kids. Longed for the smell of something simmering all day on the woodstove. Missed the magic Mama made out of mashed po-tatoes. Her gravy was just a little flour, little milk, salt, pep-per, and some drippings, but, boy, was it ever good.

I'd be there for Christmas, were it not for the *Oklahoma*.

I tried not to think about that. Instead, I lay under the stars, counting my blessings, the way Mama had taught me. There was a lot to be thankful for. And that evening, the night of December 6, 1941, the more I counted, the more blessed I felt.

Going home for Christmas would have to wait, at least for now. Maybe next year. I looked up at the sky. It was so serene, and my thoughts drifted away from home, back to the harbor.

I felt like the luckiest boy from Red Cloud, Nebraska. I was in the Navy, seeing the world, stationed in one of the most beautiful parts of that world. I was nineteen. My entire life stretched before me. The whole shimmering Milky Way of it.

And somewhere in that night, a band was playing.

4

December 7th

As daylight broke, the sun with its rays bore an almost theatrical semblance to the naval flag of Empire. Fuchida was so thrilled that he half stood up, as if to honor the beloved symbol. He looked behind him and saw his huge air armada following him in perfect formation, the sun flashing silver from its wings. For a full two or three minutes he watched the magnificent scene. O glorious dawn for Japan! he thought, in a surge of pride in his country, his men, and his mission.

—Gordon W. Prange

While we slept . . .

3:57 A.M.

Outside the entrance to Pearl Harbor

In Gordon Prange's book, *At Dawn We Slept,* the foremost Pearl Harbor scholar noted that the minesweeper *Condor* was on patrol one and three quarters miles beyond the entrance buoys to the harbor, when Ensign R. C. McCloy, who was the officer of the deck, sighted something in the darkness "about fifty yards ahead of the port bow." The officer asked Quartermaster Uttrick what he thought the object was. Peering through his binoculars, Uttrick said: "That's a periscope, sir, and there aren't supposed to be any subs in this area." McCoy sent a message by yardarm blinker to the USS *Ward,* the destroyer that was on entrance patrol, to investigate. The message read: "Sighted submerged submarine on westerly course, speed 9 knots."

The commander of the *Ward,* Lieutenant William Outerbridge, spent the next hour conducting a sonar search of the area, but he could not locate the sub.

A little after 5:00 A.M.

**Overhanging deck of the Sixth Division
on the USS *Arizona***

I awoke on my cot, about an hour and a half before sunrise. I stretched, rubbed the sleep from my eyes, and folded up my cot. I stored it in the incinerator room, then went below to shower. Afterward I dressed for the day in the typical casual clothes that sailors wore on Sundays—a clean pair of pressed white shorts and a white T-shirt, along with my sailor's hat.

5:30 A.M.
On board the USS *Arizona*
Reveille sounded over the intercom, and the ship stirred to life. Belowdecks, men tumbled out of their hammocks and headed to the showers.

5:50 A.M.
Open waters, 220 miles north of Oahu
A Japanese armada under the command of Admiral Isoroku Yamamoto and Vice Admiral Chuichi Nagumo had gathered. The attack force consisted of six aircraft carriers, two battle-ships, two heavy cruisers, one light cruiser, nine destroyers, seven tankers, and three submarines that escorted the carriers. Nagumo turned his six carriers east into the wind and increased their speed to 24 knots.

Between 6:10 and 6:20 A.M.
Japanese carriers launched 181 planes from their decks, each plane taking its place in formations that became thin lines scrawled against the rising sun. The lines read like a fore-boding prophecy on its way to fulfillment, one dark line after another, after another, after another. The first wave of planes

included 51 dive bombers, 40 torpedo bombers, 49 horizontal bombers, and 43 fighters.

6:30 A.M.
Pearl Harbor
Chow call sounded, and I ate with the other men in my group. Typical Sunday fare: coffee, powdered eggs with ketchup, fried Spam, pancakes. There were a few local items, too, mostly fruit, such as oranges and berries. It was a leisurely breakfast, which was what was so great about Sundays aboard ship.

Ours was one of 185 ships of the U.S. Pacific Fleet and auxiliary ships that were moored in the harbor that morning. In all, there were 8 battleships, 12 heavy cruisers, 9 light cruisers, 53 destroyers, and a number of auxiliary vessels like tankers, repair ships, and a hospital ship. The 3 aircraft carriers in the fleet had been scheduled to be in the harbor, but because of poor weather, they remained at sea.

6:45 A.M.
Outside the entrance to Pearl Harbor
The USS *Ward* fired on the unidentified sub. The first shot from the 4-inch guns went high, but the second struck the sub at the waterline. The sub sank, and the destroyer finished her by dropping depth charges, after which a black oil slick three hundred yards astern could be spotted.

7:00 A.M.

The *Ward* reported the sinking of the submarine to authorities at Pearl, but the report was passed so slowly up the chain of command that no alert was given to the other ships in the harbor.

Shortly after 7:00 A.M.

Opana Point Radar Station,
overlooking Oahu's north shore

Two army privates, Joseph Lockard and George Elliot, just completed their 4:00 A.M.–7:00 A.M. shift, but Lockard agreed to give the more inexperienced Elliot additional training on the equipment while they waited for the truck that would take them to breakfast. During this time, a large blip appeared on the radar screen. At first he thought the equipment was faulty, but after studying the large mass, he concluded it was a formation of planes approaching Oahu and 132 miles to the north.

Also shortly after 7:00 A.M.

Japanese carriers launched the second wave of planes, which included 77 dive bombers, 36 fighters, and 54 horizontal bombers.

7:10 A.M.

Opana Point Radar Station

Private Elliot notified headquarters at Fort Shafter, but the operator told him that all Signal Corps personnel had gone for breakfast. Elliot looked at his radar screen. The blip was now one hundred miles north of Oahu and closing. At 7:20 the operator called back, and Lockard answered. His superior officer, Lieutenant Kermit Tyler, was on the line and told him that a squadron of B-17s was scheduled to arrive at Pearl Harbor that morning from the West Coast, and not to be alarmed because it had to be them. Lochard was not convinced. A heated exchange followed. But realizing the lieutenant wouldn't budge, Lochard backed down. The two privates then turned off the radar and went to breakfast.

7:40 A.M.

The skies above Oahu

Captain Mitsuo Fuchida led the first wave of Japanese planes over the mountains along the north shore of Oahu. Nine minutes later, Fuchida's radioman signaled "To, To, To," repeating the first syllable of the Japanese word for "charge," signaling for the attack on Pearl Harbor to begin.

7:51 A.M.

Wheeler Field

Japanese Zeros attacked aircraft, hangars, and other buildings on the airstrip.

7:53 A.M.

Kaneohe and Ewa Mooring Mast Field

Enemy planes struck the airstrip, as Fuchida radioed on broadband so all could hear, "Tora, Tora, Tora," which meant a "lightning attack," alerting his superiors that their attack by surprise had been achieved.

7:55 A.M.

Pearl Harbor

Prep for morning colors sounded. At the start of each day, a signalman in the Pearl Harbor tower raised a white and blue "prep" flag. This signaled the color guards on the ships to raise the American flag, usually accompanied by each vessel's band playing the national anthem. Ours had assembled in formation on the back of the fantail, like they did every morning. They never got a day off, not even Sundays.

While I was belowdecks, color guards had assembled on the decks of 8 battleships, 8 cruisers, 29 destroyers, and a variety of support ships that made up half of the Pacific Fleet. Seven of the battleships were moored on Battleship Row,

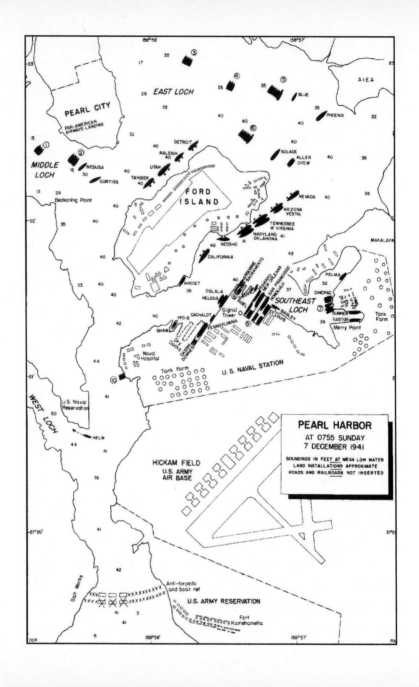

along the southeast shore of Ford Island. Ford was a small island in the harbor, cut in half by a runway. On either side of the runway were hangars, along with support facilities for the Navy planes located there. The *Arizona* was sandwiched between the island on one side and the repair ship, *Vestal,* on its seaward side.

After breakfast, I saw a box of oranges, so I turned my sailor's cap inside out and filled it with them to bring to my buddy from Arkansas, Harl, who was in sick bay with jaundice. I walked to my locker, located in the bakery passageway. Then I passed through the No. 2 casement to the forecastle deck. As I stepped into the sunshine, Harl's oranges fell from my cap. . . .

I heard the drone of aircraft engines and bombs exploding on Ford Island. A commotion at the bow, several men pointing and yelling.

"They're bombing the water tower on Ford Island!" someone hollered.

Several of us on deck ran to the bow in time to see our planes on the runway bursting into flames, and the water tower toppling over.

What the hell is going on? I asked myself.

The men were now pointing overhead and shouting. Craning my neck, I recognized the red "meatballs" on the silver wings of the planes doing the bombing: Japanese Zeros, emblazoned with the nation's "Rising Sun" disk. The sky bristled with them, circling in figure eights like birds of prey, waiting their turn to swoop down.

We all ran to our battle stations. I sped up steel ladders, my hands flying over the polished handrails that led to the sight-setter in the port antiaircraft director, which was *my* station. A Zero skimmed the surface of the harbor like a dragonfly, just twenty feet from the water, dropped its torpedo, then pulled up sharply. Pearl was a shallow harbor, varying in depth somewhere between forty and fifty feet, but standard torpedoes plunge to a depth of 150 feet before rising to attack depth. The Japanese knew if they used such a torpedo, it would dolphin, so to speak, hitting the surface and arcing downward before it stabilized its trajectory in a straight line toward its target. This would result in the torpedo hitting the muddy bottom and becoming embedded in it. Because of this, they modified it, adding wooden fins that acted as aerodynamic stabilizers, which were shed once the torpedo hit the water.

Their engineers got it right: as I was running, I felt a wallop on the ship's hull, followed by a muffled explosion deep in its bowels. The torpedo shook me but didn't slow my pace. I raced up the ladder to the radio shack, from there up another ladder to the signal bridge, up a third ladder to the bridge, and finally up a fourth ladder to the sky control platform.

I looked over my shoulder to take in the sweep of the harbor, which was in chaos. A Zero bore down on us, strafing our sailors and splintering our deck. It flew so low I could see the pilot in his leather helmet and goggles taunting me with a smirk and a wave as he passed, like a grinning devil.

The air defense alarm sounded, sending the top gunners to their stations. Shortly after that, general quarters sounded: "Attention! Attention! Attention! Man your battle stations! This is no drill! This is no drill!"

The deck was a frenzy of sailors running every which way. The band members, like the rest of the crew, ran to their battle station, in the ammunition hold several decks below. They would have gone to their assigned places, loading shells and bags of powder onto hoists that took them to the main guns on Nos. 1 and 2 turrets. The hoists were electrically operated, and it was the job of the band members to stand on either side of them to ensure that the bags of powder didn't become dislodged, jammed, or snagged as they ascended. If they did, the black powder could spill out of them and create a hazard if a spark were to ignite it.

As Lauren Bruner raced up the same ladder I had taken, a Zero fixed its sights on him. A blast from its guns, and bullets bit metal. One of those shots struck flesh, hitting the back of Lauren's lower leg. He limped onto the sky platform, a trail of blood following him. The others of our team came after him, spilling into the metal enclosure, called the "director," where we directed the antiaircraft guns—Harold Kuhn, Russell Lott, Earl Riner, George Hollowell, Alvin Dvorak, Fred Zimmerman, and Frank Lomax.

I was frantically setting the dials in the director that engaged the gears to set the sights of the antiaircraft guns. Behind each of them was a ready box of ammunition, which only held twenty-five rounds. We immediately loaded the ammo and started firing at the dive bombers. But they were flying so low we risked hitting the *Vestal* on one side of us and our own men on Ford Island on the other.

We turned our sights on the high-altitude bombers and fired at a 90-degree angle. When the crewmen loaded the guns, the gunnery officer peered through a portal and set the range and path of the target. I cranked the gauge in front of him and yelled the coordinates to the gun below.

We sent volley after volley of antiaircraft fire their way, the shells filling the sky with puffs of black smoke. Antiaircraft shells didn't explode on impact like other rounds. They had fuses inside them, that could be set to explode, say, fifteen seconds after it left the muzzle of the gun. If you found the shells were exploding too low, you adjusted the next ones to go off twenty or twenty-five seconds after they were shot from the gun.

No matter the adjustments we made, though, the Japanese bombers were too high, and our shells just couldn't touch them. It was like boxing an opponent whose reach was twice what yours was. No matter how many times you swung or how hard, you could never hit back. All the while, you were getting pummeled. The beating we took, it was brutal. We took so many hits, and not just *our* ship. . . .

There were hatches in the antiaircraft director that you could unbolt to see out, and from that hatch I watched torpedo planes flying over the sub base, circling, then coming straight down Battleship Row. I observed the *Tennessee* and the *West Virginia* take hits. I witnessed the *Oklahoma* lurch to one side, then roll over and capsize. I saw a fireball in the drydock where the *Pennsylvania* was.

The entire fleet was being destroyed before my eyes. Bombs were going off everywhere. Great billows of smoke were eating up the blue sky and turning it black. Torpedoes slammed against our hulls, spewing geysers of water into the air. Ships were taking on water, listing, capsizing. And from those ruptured ships spilled oil that congealed when it hit the water and caught fire. It seemed the whole harbor was in flames, a spreading lake of fire. The hellish sight of blacks and reds and yellows, devouring everything. The sulfurous smell of burning fuel. The acrid smell of exploding gunpowder.

And the noise, it was deafening. One explosion followed another, and after each one you could hear twisted metal writhing, letting out the most wretched sound, as if it were in agonizing pain. The whine of plane engines crisscrossed around you. As soon as one dive bomber dropped its tor-

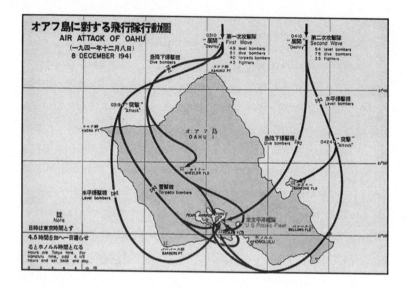

pedo, it pulled up sharply or winged off to one side, while another plane swooped down to strafe us. Machine gun bullets ricocheted off metal. The screams of our men, their bodies engulfed in flames. And the fury of our own antiaircraft guns, reverberating inside our metal cubicle so loudly I felt my eardrums were going to burst.

With each bomb that hit us, the ship shuddered. One hit No. 3 turret, but it didn't explode, careening instead into the sea. Lucky for us. Another penetrated the aft deck, but it didn't explode, either. Another stroke of luck, or so I thought until a burst of machine gun fire hammered the metal encasement on the starboard side, where Hollowell sat slumped in his chair, part of his skull blown away.

The whistling of another bomb, and we braced for impact. But it hit the *Vestal* instead. It seemed to catch much of the fury that had been aimed at the *Arizona*. The repair ship was in flames, and its crew was furiously trying to extinguish them.

As it burned, a bomb went through our aft, near the propeller, but it didn't explode. Another stroke of fortune. But I knew our luck was running out.

Yet another bomb came whistling down, and we felt a hard smack against the aft. The weapon penetrated the deck, exploding in a meat locker.

We were sitting ducks. Not just the *Arizona*, but every ship in the harbor. And there was nothing we could do about it. The dive bombers were too low for our guns, and, almost two miles above, the horizontal bombers were too high. With few exceptions, our planes, which the Japanese strategically hit first, never got a chance to get off the ground. We couldn't even make a run for it into open waters, because it took two and a half hours for the boilers of a battleship to fire up.

And so we threw our shells into the sky, as many as we could, hoping the shrapnel might shatter a cockpit, rupture a fuel line, clip a propeller. It's all we *could* do. Shoot and hope. But almost out of ammo, we had little left to fire. And with each burst that fell short, we lost a little more hope. We were only a few minutes into the fight, but the pounding we took was relentless. The entire fleet was reeling from the blows.

Everywhere you turned there was death and destruction. It was as if the whole world was collapsing in on itself, and you were right in the middle of the implosion with nowhere to run, nowhere to hide.

One of our port guns fell silent. Out of ammo. Then another. Ensign Lomax, the officer in charge, made a run belowdecks to get more. That was the last time I saw him.

Zeros strafed the ship, their bullets ripping up the deck and shredding any sailors who were on it. With each pass, the Japanese pilot smiled or waved or made some other mocking gesture. The smug bastards. The whole lot of them were cowards and murderers. Without a declaration of war, they waged war on us. Without warning. Without mercy. Without conscience. They shot at us as if we were ducks in a barrel, enjoying it as schoolboys would an arcade game at the circus.

We took another hit, which thundered through the ship. It struck the starboard side, right beside the No. 2 turret, but it didn't explode. At the same time, I saw two torpedo wakes heading directly toward us. I braced for the impact. Which never came. *Another lucky break,* I thought. Until seconds later . . .

8:06 A.M.

A great sucking sound, like a whoosh, rocked the ship and everyone in it with concussive force. A 1,760-pound, armor-piercing bomb, dropped from ten thousand feet above, had penetrated four steel decks to the ammunition magazine. The blast blew the No. 1 turret into the air, where it came crashing back onto the deck. A plume of black smoke spewed out of the forward smokestack, and an expanding fireball shot five to six hundred feet into the air, engulfing those of us in the director.

Martin Matthews was a sailor stationed on Ford Island, but a friend of his from the *Arizona* had invited him aboard the night before. He witnessed the explosion from a mooring quay after being thrown into the water. "When the *Arizona* finally started blowing up, it was ammunition, gun lockers, and shells and fragments and pyrotechnics coming, it seemed to me, from all parts of the ship. It was a series of explosions; it wasn't just one deafening one. It came to one final one where she seemed like the middle part just raised up in the water and kind of half-buckled and then settled back down." The explosion gutted the forward decks, and the turrets and conning tower sank thirty feet into the resulting crater, drawing the mast and the funnel forward. Rear Admiral Isaac C. Kidd, who had taken a position on the signal bridge, was killed in the explosion. So was Captain Franklin Van Valkenburgh, who had been on the navigation bridge, trying to establish telephone communications with other parts of the ship.

As was the *Arizona*'s twenty-one-man band.

So too were more than a thousand sailors and Marines who were at their battle stations, defending her.

The blast blew across Ford Island, knocking people off their feet. It threw dozens of men off the *Nevada* into the harbor. "Strangely enough," wrote historian Gordon W. Prange, "the explosion that destroyed *Arizona* saved *Vestal*. The concussion put out her fires as though a giant candle-snuffer had been clapped over her. It also sent tons of debris down her decks—'parts of the ship, legs, arms and heads of men—all sorts of bodies,' even living men. The explosion flung overboard about 100 men from *Vestal*. . . ."

The force of the blast showered the decks of the *Tennessee* with tons of twisted metal, including the twisted parts of our men who, in one shearing moment, had their souls torn from them. In fact, debris from the *Arizona* that rained down on the *Tennessee* caused more damage than the two bombs dropped on her by the Japanese. The carnage rained onto other ships, onto Ford Island, onto our own ship.

Martin Matthews, who was only fifteen at the time (his dad had forged his papers, saying he was seventeen), witnessed the horrific downpour. "I remember lots of steel and everything and bodies coming down, but I can't remember if any of them actually ever hit me. Evidently, they didn't, because I didn't have a scratch on me when it was over with. But I do remember many parts of what you might call shrapnel or pieces of steel from the ship and even dismembered bodies. I saw a thigh and leg; I saw fingers; I saw hands, I saw elbows and arms. It's far too much for a young boy of fifteen years old to have seen."

The flames swallowed the foremast where we were. As they shot through the two openings of the enclosure, we shielded ourselves by taking shelter under some of the equipment, our hands covering our mouths and eyes. But the flames found us, catching us all on fire, burning off our clothes, our hair, our skin.

At the same time, men below us were struggling to escape the flames. "The view of the quarterdeck of the *Arizona*, seconds after the blast destroyed her, was terrible," remembered one of the men in my division, Clay Musick, describing the chaos he saw there. "Men stumbled, men crawled, men fell on the quarterdeck. Their clothes were burned off, leaving only the charred insoles of their shoes and the remnants of cloth in the groin and under their arms. Their skin was white, their hair burned away. Their movements were stiff and robot-like."

Men stumbled around on the deck like human torches, each collapsing into a flaming pile of flesh. Others jumped into the water. When they did, you could hear them sizzle. James Cory, one of the Marines on board, recalled what he saw from the quarterdeck: "These people were 'zombies,' in essence. They were burned completely white. Their skin was just as white as if you'd taken a bucket of whitewash and painted it white. Their hair was burned off; their eyebrows were burned off. . . . Their arms were held away from their bodies, and they were stumping along the decks." While that horrific scene was unfolding below us, billows of black smoke pushed into where we were, stinging our eyes, filling our nostrils, our throats, our lungs. We stumbled to our feet, coughing out smoke, unable to catch our breaths because the fire had also burned off our oxygen.

The compartment we were in suddenly became claustrophobic, and two of the men bolted out the door to escape. Whether they jumped off the platform or were knocked off, I didn't know. I couldn't see them—and I would never again.

As we felt our way along the metal walls, the heat scorched our palms. Before he stumbled out of the director, Russell Lott grabbed a nearby blanket and wrapped it around himself, which kept his skin from getting scorched. By now, the metal floor was so hot we could feel the heat through the soles of our shoes. Lott hopped on one foot, then the other. Soon we all were shifting our weight.

Once on the outer platform, we moved toward the ladder. But flames from the inferno below leapt up the metal steps and barred our escape. There was no way down, and the metal platform we were standing on was growing hotter by the second. If we didn't get off it, and soon, we would be cooked. Below us, where the flames were coming from, was a mixture of horror and heroism.

"The ship forward of the mainmast was an inferno," recalled my shipmate Musick:

> *Directly below, the boat deck was wrecked. Motor launches, motorboats, splintered and tossed off their ways, lay among the winches, ventilators, guns, radio antenna and other smoldering gear. Out of this chaos, rose the intact, but splinter-riddled stack. The two ships' cranes appeared untouched.*
>
> *Bullets whanged into the mainmast as the rungs of successive ladders rang to my pounding feet....*
>
> *.... I went down the starboard leg ladder.*
>
> *The Marine ahead of me burned his hands on the handrail of the ladder to the quarterdeck. I was very careful to avoid those hot handrails while running down this ladder at full speed.*
>
> *White bodies, with the pitiful charred remnants of uniforms, were stacked ... beneath the overhang of the 1.1 pompom mounts on the quarterdeck. For the first time I heard cries of men in pain.*
>
> *Lt. Commander Samuel G. Fuqua ... walked among the dead, wounded, and the wreckage, calmly directing survivors over the side.*

Fuqua stayed on board until the very end. He directed his men to fight the flames with CO_2 fire extinguishers, and he worked tirelessly to get his men off the ship and into the launches. He helped at least seventy into those small craft. He didn't shelter himself from the strafing, but was on deck with his men, helping up those who had fallen. He was a picture of strength, unruffled by the chaos surrounding him, and his example inspired others.

When Fuqua ordered Earl Pecotte, the gunner's mate, to abandon ship, the man asked, "When are you leaving, sir?"

Fuqua answered, "Not until the Japs leave."

Sergeant John Baker said of Fuqua, "His calmness gave me courage and I looked around the deck to see if I could help. To Edward Wentzlaff, he displayed a courage and bravery second to none. I am proud to say I came under his authority."

LIEUTENANT COMMANDER SAMUEL Fuqua was one of the gallant men that day. So was Boatswain's Mate Second Class Joe George.

Up where we were, there was no one directing us, no way of escape, and no hope. I looked at myself, surveying the damage the blast had inflicted. My T-shirt had caught fire, burning my arms and my back. My legs were burned from my ankles to my thighs. My face was seared. The hair on my head had been singed off, and part of my ear was gone.

I stood in a stupor and would have continued to stand there were it not for a breeze that parted the smoke, revealing a sailor from the *Vestal*. It was Joe George. He had been following orders to cut the lines that tethered his ship to the *Arizona* so they could head to open waters. Since there was no one on the *Arizona* to help on our end, he was taking a fire ax and cutting the lines on his.

We called to Joe through a seam in the smoke, motioning for him to throw us a monkey's fist, which was a lightweight heaving line knotted around a metal ball and attached to a thicker rope. It was a long shot, but our desperate idea was that if we could secure a rope between the two ships, then perhaps we could make it to the *Vestal*. As Joe rummaged for the ball, I looked at my arms. A sheath of skin from each had peeled off and was draping them. I tore off one length of skin and threw it on the floor of the platform. Then the other. The remaining tissue was a webwork of pink and white and red, some of it black, all of it throbbing.

But that didn't matter. My focus narrowed to Joe George and the ball in his hand. He threw it, but it fell short. He gathered up the line and lobbed it again. Short once more. Joe was perhaps the strongest man in the harbor, an All-Navy boxer whom I described earlier as an "ox." He was the only

man with a prayer of getting that line to us—if he couldn't
do it, then it was impossible. The reality started to sink in: we
were going to burn alive.

Joe collected the rope once more. For a third time, he
tossed it with all his strength. It sailed from one wounded
ship to another, across flames, smoke, and carnage. I tracked
it all the way and caught it in the air, pulling the smaller line
until I felt the main rope. I tied the rope to the railing, cinch-
ing it tight, and Joe secured his end.

The rope stretched seventy feet to span the water below
us, which was forty-five feet down, slicked with fuel that had
caught fire. Our only hope was to make it to the *Vestal*, hand
over hand across the rope. But the flesh had been burned off
all of our hands, and using those raw fingers and palms to
get us across the chasm that separated us would be at best
excruciating, and most likely impossible.

I looked through the smoke at the *Vestal*, my burning eyes
straining to see. Joe and his captain were engaged in some
kind of debate, a heated one, from the looks of it.

The order had been given to cut loose from the *Arizona*
and head for open water. Before Joe sent a line our way, he
had been following those instructions, using his ax to cut
the mooring lines. When the *Vestal*'s captain saw the rope
that tethered his ship to ours, he looked at us. We were a
grotesque gathering of hellish creatures. Nearly naked, our
bodies were smudges of black, patches of white, slashes of

red. Stumbling into each other on the platform. Patting out the flames on our clothes. Peeling skin from our arms. We were the walking dead, and we didn't have a chance, or so it seemed to the captain.

The first in line was Harold Kuhn, right before me. He was first because he wasn't as badly injured as the rest of us, and so he would test the rope to see if it would hold. For a breathless moment, we looked down at the flames that swept through the gap that separated the two ships. Then we looked at the captain and Joe George on the other side of the chasm. The officer barked an order, but George stood defiant, glaring at him. The officer turned and left.

Joe George waved Kuhn over. As he made his way across the rope, it started to sag. We all recoiled at the sight. It was difficult enough making the trip with a taut line. With a sagging one, it would be even more difficult because it meant the descent would be steeper and we'd have to go uphill at the end. It might even be impossible. If Kuhn couldn't make it, strong as he was, how could we in our weakened condition?

Joe called to him, and the rest of us echoed the encouragement.

"You can make it!"

"Come on now!"

"Keep going!"

He made it. Kuhn made it!

At that moment a Japanese Zero caught sight of us on

the *Arizona* side and veered our way. When we saw it bearing down on us, we all ran into the director to take cover. A spray of machine gun bullets clanged off the metal, but none of them hit us—this time. Surely the Zero would be circling back. Meanwhile the inferno below seethed, its flames climbing the ladders to reach us and sending its smoke to overwhelm us.

It was now or never.

I started hand over hand across the line, feeling a surge of adrenaline as I went. The first half was okay, and I made it to the midpoint in good time. But then the rope curved upward, and I had my full weight pulling against me.

I could feel the heat from the burning oil spill below me. The exposed tissue on my legs and arms felt the heat. The pain was excruciating. My hands, raw as they were, kept going. Somehow they kept going, one hand over the other over the other. I refused to let go. Maybe I felt I would be letting the men down if I did. They were all rooting for me. Or perhaps I kept going because if I let go, the rest might not make the attempt for fear of following my fate. I knew they *had* to get off that platform or the heat would overcome them.

Joe extended a hand and his hearty encouragement as he snatched me from the flames. I was safe, for now, but I was exhausted.

As I was catching my breath, another Zero dropped from the sky, heading straight for us. When it strafed us, we all took cover again as the sharp staccato of shells rang off the metal in rapid succession. Again, none of them hit home.

One by one, each of us miraculously made it to the other side. We hadn't fallen. And we hadn't been hit by machine gun fire. There wasn't enough adrenaline in us to get us through that ordeal. We had help from the good Lord, I'm sure of that. One thing is for certain: had Joe George not stood up for us—had he not been a rebel and refused to cut the line connecting the *Vestal* to the *Arizona*—we would have been cooked to death on that platform. If anyone deserved a Medal of Honor that day, in my opinion, it was him. And I know at least five others who would second that.

Years later, Joe was interviewed about what he did that day:

George: I was on the superstructure deck, and that was up in the area where the silvering shop was. That part of the deck was about the only part of the deck that was even with the *Arizona*. The *Arizona*, although her main deck was probably lower than ours, she drew more water. But at that particular place that these people were trying to get over, they were surrounded by fire on the *Arizona*. This was on the superstructure deck where the *Vestal* was in correspondence with the level and height of the *Arizona*. They were stranded on the ship, and they were trying to get off, and they was surrounded by fire.

[*Interviewer Ronald*] *Marcello:* And so this is when you threw the line?

George: That's correct.

Marcello: How many people came across on that line? Do you know?

George: I'll tell you, I didn't wait to see because I secured it on my ship as tight as I could. They forehanded themselves over, because I couldn't help them. I went about my business.

I have a little more to add to what Joe said. After he had thrown us the line that saved our lives, his captain came up to him and berated him for what he had done. The captain, you see, had ordered him earlier to cut all lines to the *Arizona* so they could get away from her. She was burning intensely, and he feared her blowing up again and destroying his ship.

When he came to Joe, they had a heated exchange. I heard this secondhand, but this is how the conversation went.

"Cut the line," ordered the captain.

"I'm not gonna leave those men out there." Joe stood his ground, and he pointed at us, looking straight at me.

"I'm going to court-martial you if you don't!"

"Go ahead and court-martial me then. I'm not going to leave those men to die."

The captain knew the kind of man Joe was, strong as an

ox and just as stubborn. The captain left, and Joe shouted his encouragement to each of us.

I still remember what he said when it was *my* turn. "C'mon, kid. You can make it!"

When we reached the *Vestal*, we were totally spent. We waited there for some time as Joe and several other men went about cutting the mooring lines. Before the ship left for open waters, its men urgently flagged down a passing motor launch. Cutting through the chaotic waters, the daring craft sidled up next to the *Vestal*. We *Arizona* escapees were helped into the launch, which wasted no time getting us to shore, where medical help awaited.

As I looked back at the harbor billowing furiously with smoke, seeing the Pacific Fleet destroyed where they were moored, staring at the collapsed remains of the *Arizona* engulfed in flames . . . the devastating sweep of it was too much.

At that moment, I knew I had lost a part of myself in the ruins of that ship, and a big part of my family in the men who died there. I turned my head.

I had to look away from my ship, from the once-majestic form that had taken my breath away when I first saw her; from my home, filled with so much life less than an hour before.

And I had to turn away from my shipmates, from the future that no longer awaited them . . . and from a part of myself that now would be forever entombed with them.

PART TWO

5

The Damage

Dear Lord,
Lest I continue
My complacent way,
Help me to remember that somewhere,
Somehow out there
A man died for me today.
As long as there be war,
I must answer
Am I worth dying for?

Just when it seemed as if the planes were leaving, another wave of Japanese aircraft arrived—carrying fresh bombs, torpedoes, bullets, and pilots, eager to participate in the slaughter. It was like a biblical plague. The first wave came at us relentlessly, fighters raking the decks of our ships with machine guns, other planes dropping almost to sea level, leveling off, flying broadside toward our hulls, dropping their torpedoes into the water, then peeling off before they hit. All the while, other aircraft circled high above the harbor, waiting for their time to kill.

Shortly before 10 A.M., the planes finally left. In less than two hours, they had turned the peace and calm of the harbor into a seething cauldron of smoke and fire. Lying in their wake was the wreckage of what was once the Pacific Fleet. When the smoke cleared and the fires extinguished, the destruction was staggering.

First, the property loss:

- U.S. Navy aircraft: 31 damaged; 92 destroyed
- U.S. Army Air Corps aircraft: 128 damaged; 77 destroyed
- Battleships: 6 damaged; 2 destroyed
- Cruisers: 3 damaged
- Destroyers: 3 damaged
- Auxiliaries: 4 damaged; 1 destroyed

Those figures don't include the hangars and other buildings that were ruined. In spite of how staggering the losses were, three assets were not claimed. First, our three aircraft carriers were out to sea on maneuvers, and so our airpower in the Pacific was not diminished. Second, the Japanese, inexplicably, did not strike the numerous storage tanks of oil that were there, and so our fuel supply was untouched. And third, of all the buildings the Japanese destroyed, they hadn't crippled any of the repair facilities, and so we were able to start immediately restoring the fleet.

After the attack was over, the first priority was to rescue survivors. Here is where our men were the most heroic, in my opinion. All of them were exhausted from being fired upon nonstop for almost two hours, but you never would have known it. If our men weren't in the hospitals or triage areas, they were in boats, fishing out men from the harbor, sailors covered in oil, many of them burned, wounded, in shock. Or they were putting out fires on ships so rescue efforts could be made. Others were trucking the wounded to hospitals.

It is easy to tally property losses, but how do you calculate the personal ones? A plane can be replaced; a person cannot. I'll at least try.

- U.S. Navy: 2,008 killed; 710 wounded
- U.S. Army: 218 killed; 364 wounded
- U.S. Marine Corps: 109 killed; 69 wounded
- Total killed: 2,403
- Total wounded: 1,176.

Laid out like that, in lists, the losses seem like a column on a spreadsheet, debits noted by whole numbers (deaths) and fractions (the wounded). Sometimes what remained approached zero, where there wasn't even enough left of the man's personal belongings to send home to the family. Admiral Kidd, for example. All the salvage team found of him was his Naval Academy class ring and a few brass buttons from his uniform. That was all they could return to his widow.

And what about the band? Their battle station was below on the third deck, where they manned the ammunition hoists for the big guns of the No. 2 turret. They were right in the middle of where most of the ship's gunpowder was stored, a veritable powder keg. The bomb struck a little forward of the starboard side of the No. 2 turret, penetrating four decks before exploding. They were virtually ground zero of the blast.

In one way of doing the math, it was a total loss of twenty-one men. But how do you measure the destruction of all that talent, all those dreams, all those bands that never were, the careers, the joy they might have brought to others, and all the music that, in an instant, was forever silenced?

The loss was incalculable.

All totaled, the number of sailors who died on the *Arizona* was 1,177. Nearly half of all the Americans who died that day. Gone in a blinding flash of light, an eerie whoosh, and a cascading devastation of explosions. One has only to stand in the shrine room of the USS *Arizona* Memorial, where all 1,177 names are chiseled onto a white marble wall, stained indelibly with black ink, to get a sense of the enormity of the loss.

Staggering, by any measure.

THE RESCUE WORK was hard but hopeful, and there were amazing stories of survival. The recovery work, on the other hand, well, those were stories you didn't want to talk about. One man who served on the *Arizona* for only a short time before the attack volunteered to dive and bring back bodies so they could have a proper burial. One of the remains he recovered was a friend. The body was so bloated the diver barely recognized him, and he had to cut the carcass open in order to extricate him. The ordeal shook the man to the core.

Historian Thurston Clarke cites another example of how grisly the recovery efforts were. "Sterling Cale," he writes, "was placed in charge of a six-man graves registration and burial detail that went aboard the *Arizona* on December 11. It was grim work. He wore hip waders and long leather gloves up to his elbows to do it. He saw piles of ashes here and there, and thought to himself, *My God, these were human beings!* He brushed the ashes into sea bags designated for the dead, or what was left of them. He and his team worked every day for a week. He found torsos without heads, and heads without torsos. In the fire control tower there was a three-foot-long mass of charred bodies fused together so tightly he could not make out a single individual sailor. As he tried separating the bodies, a head, or an arm, or a leg, or some other body part came off in his hands, or fell from the mass. Several times he stopped to vomit."

Up until August 1943, salvage efforts on the *Arizona* were still ongoing, as crews worked to pump water and oil out of the compartments that were accessible, bringing out any remains they could. One of the divers talked about the experience: "You couldn't see well with all that oil. I'd just stand still and eventually a skeleton would float by and tap me on the shoulder. Of course, I couldn't tell who he was, but he was probably someone I had known. Hell, we could have drunk beer together at the Black Cat or somewhere. It was horrible."

There is no way you can understand what it was like, unless you had been there. I can tell you some of the stories, but here is where we reach the limits of storytelling. Here is the place where there are no words. Perhaps that is as it should be. Maybe some horrors should be left unshared.

I HAVE TRIED my best to express what I could about what I experienced that day. It isn't enough, though, because it is only one side of the story. The other side lies an ocean away.

When you read a statistic, like 2,403 dead, it says so little. A statistical death is only the skeletal remains of a life. Without flesh and blood; its beating heart or its winking eye; its quick wit or its contagious laugh.

What I would like to do is try to breathe some life into one of those statistics. Let's start with a name: Clyde Williams, a member of the *Arizona*'s famed band. His instrument? The trumpet. A woman named T. J. Cooper compiled an encyclopedic volume of the 1,177 men of the *Arizona* who died at Pearl Harbor. Beside Clyde Williams's name is a black-and-white picture of him. Young and wholesome-looking, he is dressed in his Navy whites, a dark tie crisscrossed loosely over his chest. Handsome. His whole life just waiting for him. Here is the entry.

Williams, Clyde Richard. Musician, Second Class, Serial No: 356 42 55, US Navy. Clyde was born September 25, 1922 in Henryette, Oklahoma, the son of Richard B. Williams, Jr. and Martha Jane (Fretwell) Williams. He enlisted in the US Navy November 27, 1940 and attended the Navy School of Music in Washington, DC graduating on May 23, 1941 as a member of the USS *Arizona* Band. Clyde reported for duty on the USS *Arizona* June 17, 1941. His battle station was in the black powder room passing ammunition to the *Arizona*'s gunners during the attack. He was killed in action on December 7, 1941 at Pearl Harbor, Hawaii. Clyde was awarded the Purple Heart Medal,

American Defense Service Medal, Asiatic Pacific Campaign Medal with Bronze Star and World War II Victory Medal posthumously. He remains on duty on the USS *Arizona*. Clyde is commemorated on the USS *Arizona* Memorial and the Memorial Tablets of the Missing, National Cemetery of the Pacific, Honolulu, Hawaii. He was survived by his Father, Mr. Richard B. Williams, Jr. 1006 Griffin Street, Okmulgee, Oklahoma.

That is something, certainly, but not enough for us to feel the loss of who he was. Fortunately, he wrote letters home, which his family saved. Here is a postcard he sent that has a picture of the USS *Arizona* on it. Postmark: June 21, 1941, Long Beach, California.

Dear Folks, This is the ship that our band is on for permanent duty. She is painted battleship grey now. She is a good ship and the officers and crew are all swell. They say that they enjoy our music and want us to play all the time.

I don't know where we are going, but we'll get there.

Take care of everything and I might be home this year or next.

Love, Proke [his nickname]

Another postcard, this time to his sister Molly. It has a picture of Hawaii on one side. Postmark: July 11, 1941. Honolulu, Hawaii.

Dear Molly, This is it. Hawaii, I mean. The Isle of Dreams.
It is really a wonderful country and lots of beautiful scenery
all around.

I may be home around Christmas or sometime next year.

Tell Mate and Pate [mother and father] "hello" and ask
Pate if he got the money orders from Long Beach and here. I
am still holding on to the stubs. Let me know if anything goes
wrong. Love, Proke

When Molly first heard the news about the bombing of
Pearl Harbor, she bought a spiral notebook to keep a daily
record of her thoughts. She planned to read it to her brother
when he came home; she thought they would have a good
laugh over how much the family worried about him.

This record is indicative of what 2,403 families were going through at the time, not hearing anything definite about
their sons. It shows the various emotions they experienced,
from denial to anxiety to fear to anger to some place of res-
ignation, and finally to a place of resolve. The main emotion she and her whole family went through was denial. How
could God allow something this bad to happen to such good
people? *His* people?

Sunday, December 7, 1941—*I stayed all Saturday night with*
Kay and Margaret Mary. They got up early and went to Tulsa.
Everyone was in the best of spirits.

I was at Mary's when the announcement came that Japan was bombing Pearl Harbor and Manila. My brother is in the Harbor, in the U.S. Navy on board the USS Arizona. *When I heard the announcement, I grabbed my coat and ran all the way home.*

All afternoon we stayed by the radio. We had a radio in the front room, kitchen, and bedroom, each on a different station. We heard the USS West Virginia *was sunk, and I know two sailors on that ship.*

Japan had attacked us with no warning, and later in the afternoon she declared war on the U.S. The president will meet with the House and Senate tomorrow.

I had a date tonight with Vinny, but no one felt much like having fun. We all feel nothing but hatred for Japan. Everyone is worried about his or her son.

People have been very nice to us, calling to see if we have heard anything about Clyde. All we know is that Pearl Harbor is greatly damaged and Hickam Field (an Army air field in Hawaii) reports 350 boys killed in one barracks.

All we can do is wait.

Monday, December 8, 1941—So *many false reports are coming through that we are beginning to believe only official reports. The president asked Congress to declare war, and a few hours later, both House and Senate declared war on Japan. Only one vote was cast against war, by Jeannette Rankin of Montana, in the House. Public opinion is very marked against* *her, because our nation is certainly not going to stand by and let Japan or any country do such a dirty trick to us!*

Germany will probably declare war on us, but we expected that.

The nations are all lining up. They predict that all nations will be in before long.

We still have no word from Clyde. Mother heard that all families have been notified if their sons were killed, so she feels a little better.

Tuesday, December 9, 1941—*Still no word about Clyde. They tell us that "no news is good news," so we try to keep cheerful. Some families are acting so silly! They try to call, cable, or wire their sons, but no messages are being put through. My goodness, if everyone did that, the official messages couldn't get through.*

New York City had an air raid practice today, and California had one last night. They prepared to black out the White House today.

Had a date with J.B. tonight, and we listened to the president's speech in the kitchen of a honky-tonk. He said he feels great concern about the families of the boys, and we will be notified as soon as possible.

There is still no report of the USS West Virginia.

Mother spent all day Sunday and Monday crying and Daddy spent it cussing!

Wednesday, December 10, 1941—*The Japs claimed today to have sunk the USS* Enterprise. *Two of our Okmulgee boys are on it. The report on it and on the* West Virginia *are still unofficial.*

We still haven't heard from Clyde.

All the cities on the West Coast are blacked out tonight. A Japanese air raid is expected in twelve hours. Enemy planes are hovering near the coastline.

These are awful times for all of us.

Thursday, December 11, 1941—*Germany and Italy declared war on us today, and we returned the compliment. Still no news from Clyde.*

Friday, December 12, 1941—*Still no news from Clyde! I think I could break down and cry for about an hour, and have hysterics and scream, I'd feel better. I haven't cried yet. After all, I have faith in God and I know he will bring Clyde safely through.*

A little boy about ten years old went to the recruiting office somewhere today, and told the officer he wanted to enlist. The officer asked him if he thought he could whip the Japs. The boy said, "No, you have enough big guys to do that. But those Japs have little boys, and I can whip all the little Japs."

That shows how we Americans feel!

Saturday, December 13, 1941—*Daddy goes to work every morning at five o'clock, and at five-thirty Mother woke me* *up crying and practically having hysterics! I rushed into her bedroom, and they had just announced that the Japs claim to have sunk the* Arizona, *the ship Clyde is on. They kept saying the report was not confirmed at Washington, so I finally convinced her that it was probably just a scheme to find out where the* Arizona *was, as it is the flagship of the fleet.*

Sunday, December 14, 1941—*Went to church and then came home. Pate [father] told me the radio had announced that the War Department had neither confirmed or denied that the* Arizona *had sunk.*

Monday, December 15, 1941—*The first half of today was very peaceful. We heard that Sec. Knox had arrived in Washington this morning. Then—! Aunt Sarah called from Tulsa to say that Knox had released his report and the* Arizona *and four destroyers were sunk. There were 2,684 killed, ninety-one officers killed and 678 wounded.*

We still haven't heard from Clyde.

There are nearly fifty missing. Of course, if they are dead, the parents have probably been notified, so we are sure he is alive. But there is no way of knowing if he is wounded. He must be, 'cause he hasn't written us. This has been the longest day I have ever lived through!

Our relatives have been so kind, to say nothing of our friends. Our aunts and uncles have telegramed [sic], called long-distance, and written to see if we have heard anything. The phone has been hot all evening!

I'm afraid we won't have a very Merry Christmas this year.

Tuesday, December 16, 1941—Still no news from Clyde. People have been calling all day to encourage us. This book helps a lot to unburden myself.

Wednesday, December 17, 1941—Now I know how it feels to have a broken heart! Pate told me tonight that I had better prepare for the worst. He said he gave up yesterday and fully expects to get bad news tonight or tomorrow. The ship went so fast that there is no way that we can see for any of them to get off.

The Nesbitt boy's parents received word today that their son is missing.

I don't think I can **stand** this!

Thursday, December 18, 1941—We still haven't heard, so our hopes are getting up a little. We figure the government would have let us know by now.

This suspense is terrible!

Friday, December 19, 1941—Still no word! The rumor about the Nesbitt boy is false—he is okay.

Saturday, December 20, 1941—Pate got the telegram at eight-thirty, and told us at nine o'clock.

Clyde is dead!

The telegram lists him as missing, because he went down with the ship and his body was not recovered.

I don't think I can stand it!

The telegram:

KM108 71 GOVT=WASHINGTON DC 20 651P

[The date of receipt, 1941 Dec 20 PM 7 23, was stamped in the upper-right-hand corner. The Xs stand for periods.]

RICHARD B WILLIAMS JR=
1006 GRIFFIN ST
THE NAVY DEPARTMENT DEEPLY REGRETS TO
INFORM YOU THAT YOUR SON CLYDE RICHARD
WILLIAMS MUSICIAN SECOND CLASS US NAVY IS
MISSING FOLLOWING ACTION IN THE PERFORMACE
[*sic*] OF HIS DUTY AND IN THE SERVICE OF HIS
COUNTY [*sic*] X THE DEPARTMENT APPRECIATES
YOUR GREAT ANXIETY AND WILL FURNISH YOU
WITH FURTHER INFORMATION PROMPTLY WHEN
RECEIVED X TO PREVENT POSSIBLE AID TO OUR
ENEMIES PLEASE DO NOT DIVULGE THE NAME OF
HIS SHIP OR STATION=
REAR ADMIRAL RANDALL JACOBS CHIEF OF
THE BUREAU OF NAVIGATION

The house was full of friends until midnight, and Aunt Lola, Uncle Sylvester, Grandma and Grandpa, and Aunt Hazel are on their way [from Texas].

We will never get over this!

The next day, Molly's dad wrote a letter to the editor of their local newspaper.

Mr. Joe Croom, Editor

The Okmulgee Times

Dear Mr. Croom,

We received a message last Saturday night, Dec. 20, from the United States Navy, stating that our son and brother, Clyde Richard Williams, is missing following action in the performance of his duty and in the service of his country.

That can mean only one thing in this particular case— Clyde went down with his ship and his body was not recovered.

To us that was a terrific blow—a blow from which we all will never completely recover—a blow that has us, for the moment, floored.

But, with the help of God and the hundreds of friends here in Okmulgee, we will not stay down for the count. We can't stay down because we, like every other citizen of Okmulgee, have a job to do.

One very important thing for all of us here in Okmulgee is to have courage. If we do not have courage, how can we ex-

pect our servicemen to have courage? And without courage a serviceman is worthless. Yes, above all, we must have courage and faith.

Another job we have to do is to help our government furnish our servicemen with arms, ammunition, clothing, and food, without which they can never win the war. This we will do by buying all the defense stamps and bonds we can. We know that if Clyde could speak to all of his friends today, he would say, "This do in remembrance of me."

So let us all put our shoulder to the wheel and push a little harder, and win this war so Clyde's death will not have been in vain.

To our many friends who are standing by, ready and willing to assist us in any way we may need assistance, we are indeed grateful.

Sincerely,
JANE, DICK, AND RUTH MAE WILLIAMS.

Clyde Williams. Now you know something of the man behind the name. Now you appreciate what his loss meant to so many who loved him. Behind every name on that marble wall at the USS *Arizona* Memorial is a person who meant something to someone, who meant the world to someone. Several someones, in all likelihood. When he died, their worlds collapsed. And though in time their wounds would be healed, they would never again be whole.

Only someone who has lost a child or had a loved one taken too soon knows what that is like.

THE FINAL COMPETITION for the 1941 Battle of Music was never held. Because of that, Fleet Recreation asked all the bands still in Hawaii to vote for the band they thought was the best for that year.

The outcome was unanimous—the USS *Arizona* band.

Sometime later, the band members' families were notified that the trophy for the contest had been named after their band. Shortly after that, on April 2, 1942, the Navy released the following story, which was carried in newspapers from coast to coast.

What became of the boys in the band when the guns began to roar?

Many a civilian has asked that question. Blowing a horn or beating a drum is not firing a gun. What becomes of the ship's musicians when the battle rages?

The most dramatic answer to that question has been furnished by the incident of the ship's band of the battleship *Arizona*.

On December 7 they went to their battle station, one of the most hazardous on the ship—down below, passing ammunition to the guns above.

To a man, the *Arizona*'s band was killed when the battleship's magazine exploded.

Great interest in the trophy has been expressed by the U.S. Navy School of Music at Washington, and in response to its request, a picture of the trophy was painted by Alfred DuPont, illustrator at the fleet recreation office, and sent to the national capital to be placed on permanent exhibit there.

Henceforth the trophy will be known as the *Arizona* trophy.

After the war, it will be put up again to be challenged, when the Battle of Music will be resumed.

All the families were sent a picture of the trophy. I'll take a shot at describing it. It has the Statue of Liberty holding a blazing torch and standing on a bronze base, which bears the following inscription: "Grand Prize, Battle of Music, United States Navy 1941." Two eagles flank the inscription, their wings outstretched. A bronze plate is attached to the base of the trophy. It reads: "1941 Winning Orchestra 1941. *USS Arizona*. Sic Itur Ad Astra. F. W. Kinney, Bandmaster." The Latin phrase—*Sic Itur Ad Astra*—literally means: "Such is the way to the stars." It is an ancient way of saying, "the way to immortality." Below the name of the bandmaster are the twenty names of the *Arizona*'s band.

Gallant men, every one of them.

ELEANOR ROOSEVELT, WIFE of the president, carried a wallet that now resides in the Roosevelt Presidential Library. It may seem hard to imagine why an insignificant accessory like that would have been deemed significant enough to be put on display so future generations could see it.

What was so special about it?

A wallet was a fairly common accessory for women in that time period, so it's not a rare item by any means. Nothing in its external appearance stands out. It wasn't made by a famous designer. In fact, it's quite plain—rectangular in shape, red in color, made out of leather.

Inside Eleanor's wallet there is a folded-up piece of paper, yellowed with age, its creases well worn, as if it had been unfolded often, then refolded and placed back in the wallet.

On the paper is a poem, the same one that opens this chapter. It ends:

Somehow out there
A man died for me today.
As long as there be war,
I must answer
Am I worth dying for?

Eleanor put it in her wallet after December 7, and she was determined to carry it with her until the war ended. As it turned out, she kept it in that wallet for the rest of her life.

The poem is displayed near the *Arizona* Memorial, inscribed on a metal plaque that is embedded in a low, rectangular stone along a path that looks out to the sunken ship.

If you were there on that path, looking out to the sunken remains of what was once the pride of the Pacific Fleet, it would be hard not to pray, not to realize how complacently we live our day-to-day lives, hard not to ask God for forgiveness for our forgetfulness. We have forgotten so much, not just individually but as a nation.

A *man* died for me today.

That sailor, soldier, or Marine was someone's son, brother, husband, perhaps, or someone's father, nephew, cousin, friend.

A man *died* for me today.

Two thousand, four hundred and three men perished at Pearl Harbor, 1,177 from the *Arizona* alone. Each of those individuals had a name, all of which are on display in the solemn shrine that stands above that ship.

A man died *for me* today.

He was there, on that ship, scrubbing the decks, painting the steel, running the drills, and learning the skills to defend us, you and me. This is what freedom costs. And these are the men who helped pay for it. Giving up their dreams, so *we* could have a future. Sacrificing their lives, so *we* could live.

Of all the questions we could ask of God in times of war—from the protection we ask for our loved ones to the clarification we ask as to the why of it all—there is one we should not direct to Him but to ourselves.

Am I worth dying for?

Am I worth the sacrifice of who *they* were or someday would become? I've reflected on this question every day since December 7, 1941.

Am I?

6

Among Angels

Men of the Navy Medical Department at Pearl Harbor were just as surprised as other Americans when the Japanese attacked on the morning of 7 December 1941, and, like other men of the Navy and Marine Corps at Pearl Harbor, they were momentarily stunned by the blow. From their first realization of an enemy attack, however, the doctors, dentists, nurses, and corpsmen were unexcelled in personal bravery, in determination, in resourcefulness, and in their capacity to put into practice previously formulated plans.
—Navy Medical Department Preparedness, December 1941

Pulling away from the *Vestal* on the morning of December 7, the motor launch that ferried us survivors across the harbor ran full bore, its bow slapping hard against the water, flouncing us along the way. Some men in that launch were taken to the floating hospital on the harbor, the USS *Solace*.

The *Solace* had four lifeboats in the water, skimming sailors from the sea of congealed oil that surrounded them. In places the oil was one to two feet deep. Some of the men were pulled out, black as soot; the white of their eyes flashed as they opened them. Others were hauled out and their skin slipped away as if it had been blanched right off them. And then there were the nameless, faceless others who bobbed in the oil slicks like charred wood, all black and hard. They were left in the water, because orders had been given to just retrieve the living. Once on board, many of the living had their limbs amputated. Before long, there were so many arms and legs lying around that they started feeding them into the incinerator.

Because of the sea of flames around the *Arizona*, it was too dangerous for those boats to get close. From the looks of it, there was no need to, because there were no signs of life. And yet official records indicate that a boat from the *Solace* was scorched from those fires, while its crew, at great danger, rescued men from those waters.

Those of us who weren't taken aboard the *Solace* were dropped off on shore, where a truck was waiting to shuttle us to the Naval Hospital on Oahu. A couple of men on shore helped us off the motor launch and into the back of an open-air truck, where a number of other sailors had already been picked up. They lay there, gritting their teeth to bite back the pain. Those without burns were on the floor of the truck, cradling their wounds. Those with burns stood. It was just too painful to lie down. The truck seemed to go airborne with every chuckhole it hit, and it hit a lot of them.

When we arrived at the Naval Hospital, the truck lurched to a stop. I was helped down by a couple of hospital personnel. As they helped the others off the truck, I took in the sight of so many men on cots, on blankets, stretched out on the lawn. I looked at myself, checking how severe my own injuries were. My T-shirt had been burned off, but I still had on my white shorts and black shoes. If it sounds like I'm lingering too long on my clothing, I want to share some observations from a medical report, based on the reports of the doctors who treated us.

The extent of the burns suffered by the men was determined by the amount of clothes they happened to have on at the time of the attack. Of the men who were burned, those with the least amount of clothing suffered the most extensive burns. Indeed, the correlation between the amount of uncovered body surface and the amount of body surface affected was strikingly high. Often times the burns simply followed the line of the clothing. All the doctors who reported on the Pearl Harbor burn cases remarked upon the protection that clothing offered against so-called flash burns. Even skivvy shirts, shorts, and other thin apparel served as protection against flash burns. Men who were wearing undershirts had no burns on the chest or abdomen; men who were wearing undershirts and shorts only, had burns on the face, arms, and legs; men who were completely dressed usually had only their faces and hands burned.

Nurses rushed to meet us, carrying stretchers for those who couldn't walk. Most couldn't. One of the nurses came to me, her face almost white. "Oh, my God. What happened *here?*" I must have looked like the walking dead. My skin was black, and in places it was white and pink. Seeing that my burns were seeping fluid, a nurse took gauze that had been dipped in a saline solution and patted down my burns. When the salt water hit my exposed tissue, it burned like all get-out.

As the charred and wounded started piling up outside, nurses gave shots of morphine to as many as needed it. The drug was packaged in syrettes, which were small plastic flasks equipped with hypodermic needles. A measured amount of morphine was in each flask, and this made the process of relieving pain not only safer but faster. Nurses merely put their hand in their "battle bag," pulled out one of the syrettes, removed the protective tube from the needle, and pushed a half grain of morphine into the wounded. Nurses used their lipstick to mark an *M* on the forehead of the men who had just received a shot so that another nurse wouldn't come by and give him an additional one. Too much morphine can kill a man. Besides, the supply was limited, and every ounce was needed. Nurses also used their lipstick to distinguish those who needed immediate attention from those who didn't.

I must have appeared to be someone who needed urgent attention, because immediately a gurney was rolled in front of me. I couldn't lie down, so I just sat on the edge as they pushed me inside. The doctors there were overwhelmed, so were the nurses assisting them. Around 60 percent of the men brought to the hospital suffered from burns. A third of them would die. Doctors initially treated them with an atomizer that held soothing solutions, spraying the solution directly onto the burn. The drug, sulfathiazole, was given orally to prevent germs from turning the exposed wounds into a hotbed for infection.

What remained of my clothes was cut off. After treating me, they laid me on my stomach, and I remained in that position all night, unable to move. Many of the men in the ward were in worse shape than I was; there were so many of them that the nurses couldn't keep up. The men yelled and screamed, calling for the nurses, for their mothers, for God.

MANY OF THE men who were brought to the hospital had severe burns over half of their bodies. The particular problem these men faced was that their own plasma, which is the watery portion of the blood, was being sent to the blistered or raw areas of their bodies in order to protect the exposed tissue. Their burns could drain the body's supply of plasma so fast that it could cause the body to go into shock. And almost every patient suffered from shock, in some degree or another. When the body's plasma is low, it restricts circulation, depriving the cells of oxygen. Without oxygen, the cells begin to die.

Before the first wave of the attack was over, a trickling of casualties appeared at various medical facilities on the island. Soon the trickle became a stream; the stream, a torrent. Before long, each facility was running low on blood. That is when Dr. Forrest J. Pinkerton, who had been making his rounds at Queen's Hospital, heard the call for plasma from Tripler Hospital. He rushed to the refrigeration plant of the Hawaiian Electric Company, where the blood supply was stored. There were only 210 flasks of plasma, each containing half a pint. The flasks were distributed as equitably as possible. Realizing the need for more blood, Dr. Pinkerton raced to the radio station and walked up three flights of stairs. He paused to catch his breath, then broadcast this simple appeal: "A call for volunteer blood donors! Report immediately to Queen's Hospital!"

In half an hour, four hundred people had arrived, standing in line at the hospital's entrance. They came from all walks of life. Honolulu society women showed up and stood next to the city's lower classes. The wife of a corporate president waited next to a waterfront washerwoman. The Japanese who lived on the island showed up in droves. A Portuguese mother brought her nineteen-year-old blind son, along with her sixteen-year-old blind daughter. Defense workers left their jobs, all grimy, gave blood, then returned to work. Welders came, along with fieldworkers. Employers bused their employees there. The crew from a Dutch ship, there for only a few hours, came to give blood. So did six husky Dutch women.

A number of donors came back twice in the same day. When a nurse recognized one second-class seaman who was in line for his second donation, she chided him: "You shouldn't come back so soon."

"My brother was killed," he explained. "I want to do something."

His words captured the mood of the entire city. "I want to do something." Among those who needed to act were the women from Hotel Street, the road that was synonymous with prostitution. The establishments had exotic-sounding names like Tin Can Alley, Blood Town, Mosquito Flats, Hell's Half Acre. And sailors stood in line for their turn with the women who worked there. Sometimes the lines were double, stretching around the block.

This time, the women of Hotel Street were the ones waiting in line, eager to offer their arms to the needle and give their blood. After donating, several of them asked what else they could do. They were given jobs washing tubing in the laboratory, which was the dirtiest and smelliest work in the hospital. I don't know how they felt about that. My guess is they were glad they could help, maybe even honored.

A newspaper reporter with the byline "Hotel Street Harry" wrote the following commendation for those women: "As the Japanese planes were still dropping their bombs, the working women of Hotel Street became unexpected and much needed first responders, rushing to Hickam Field and Pearl Harbor to help thousands of wounded Americans. The women, comfortable dealing with intimate situations, bandaged and nursed the men and donated gallons of their blood (which the Army doctors knew was clean). And with the overflow of patients and shortage of hospital beds on Oahu, the women of Hotel Street gave up their own rooms, turning the brothels into hospital wards. For this selfless action way beyond the call of duty, the Ladies of Hotel Street earned the lasting admiration, respect and loyalty of the men of the United States Armed Forces."

IF YOU LOOKED toward the harbor on that first night after the attack, you could see flames from the *Arizona* lighting up the night sky. Fearing another assault, the hospital was blacked out by putting dark curtains or black paper over the windows and turning off the lights. With the lights all turned off, the staff had to use flashlights to get around. They even used them during surgery.

Between ten and eleven o'clock that night planes could be heard flying overhead. All the flashlights were turned off, and for a few terrifying minutes everything was dark, and still, and quiet. One by one, the flashlights came back on, and everyone at the hospital returned to work.

Of that first night, my memory is filled with pain. If I tried to move, even an inch, the pain was unbearable. I also remember how horrible the smell was. I had terrible nightmares where I relived the attack, and I remember a couple of times waking up screaming. And if my own cries didn't wake me up, those of others did. So many of them just wanted to be put out of their misery. I heard a sailor, a few beds down, call to a nurse, "Hit me in the head with your flashlight and knock me out. Please." It wasn't a joke. Others called out, wanting someone to just shoot them. That's how bad the pain was.

It had been a long day for the doctors and nurses. The medical officer in command of the hospital made a tally: "At least 490 men were treated during the day of December 7th in the wards, and from 200–300 received first aid treatment but were not admitted. . . . There are records of 482 men dead upon admission to the wards." When the bed count was made at midnight, the hospital held 960 men.

Besides the care given us from the medical staff, three things got us through the night: morphine, sulfa drugs, and plasma. Even so, not everyone made it. The next morning, several of the men were dead. Their bodies were covered, then taken away by orderlies and stacked in a pile like cordwood. The doctors made their rounds, checking on us. They only had time for a cursory look and a few words of instruction to the nurses who were caring for us.

Burn patients were treated in a number of different ways, depending on the doctor or on what supplies were most readily available. Tannic acid was most routinely used, either in a gel form or in solution. Picric acid and sulfanilamide powder were also employed, along with gentian violet and the triple dye, which sometimes had silver nitrate in it. Gauze pads soaked in mineral oil and sulfa drugs that were applied to the burned area was another way of treating the burn patients.

Most of the injured had lost blood, and almost everywhere you looked, men were receiving transfusions. They needed a full supply of blood because blood brought oxygen to the open wounds and helped them heal faster.

Mercifully, I don't remember a lot about those first few days. My wounds were wetted down with a solution of tannic acid, that much I do recall, and that kept them from scabbing over while helping to lower the burning sensation and to bring some measure of healing. But recovery was painfully slow. And my time in that ward seemed an eternity.

Doctors came and went, and I don't remember much about them. I don't recall much about the chaplains, either. They generally steered clear of the burn ward, because the stench was so awful. The nurses, though, I can't forget. They somehow endured the smell. Maybe they became used to it. No, no one gets accustomed to the smell of burnt flesh. However they managed it, they did their lifesaving work with such effortless grace, with beautiful gentleness and kindness, that at times it felt as if you were being attended by angels.

A man would call to one of them, "Nurse! Nurse!"

Maybe he cried out because he knew he was losing the battle for his life, and he didn't want to die alone. And his nurse came, grasped his hand, kept holding it, listening to his confession, perhaps, or perhaps to his fever-induced ramblings about home, about his mother or his kid brother. And however incoherent those ramblings were, she listened, smiled, said a few soft words to salve his soul. No one should die alone. And the nurses made sure, to the best of their ability, that no one did.

One of those nurses, Rosella Asbelle, recalls what it was like to work on the burn ward. "It was really tragic. These kids were so young and so burned. . . .

"The saddest thing, though, was having night duty. That's when these severely burned kids would die. And you'd know when that was going to happen. Many a time, I'd sit by the bed of a young man, boy, who was burned, as he died talking about his family. It was generally about 4:30 or 5:30 in the morning when most of them went. You'd hold their hands and talk to them about their families."

Nurses like Rosella saw so much, including the most grotesque disfigurements anyone had ever witnessed, lying and dying before them. It must have broken their hearts. I'm sure they fell apart when they had a rare minute to themselves.

"In an hour," someone commented, "boys had become men, and men heroes." That was true not only of the sailors in the harbor but also of the men and women in the hospital. There were heroics in that hospital that never made the headlines. People there who would not have a monument erected in their honor. Who never got a medal for their valor. Or a promotion for their service. They were some of the most heroic people I have ever met. And I don't even remember their names.

The good Lord remembers them, though. I'm sure of that. He watched as they spoon-fed us. Or said a prayer on someone's behalf. Offering a hand to help them up. A bandage on the forehead, or a kiss, whichever was needed most.

7

America Responds

As Admiral Yamamoto had feared, the attack on Pearl Harbor awakened the sleeping giant, America. And the manner of the attack—which Americans regarded as a treacherous, underhanded assault—aroused the country's patriotism to unimagined heights. The phrase "Remember Pearl Harbor" immediately became a rallying cry, as young men flocked to enlist and those who stayed behind bought war bonds and volunteered in various ways to help the war effort.

—Dan Van Der Vat,
Pearl Harbor: The Day of Infamy—An Illustrated History

As the wounded were treated in various hospitals in the area and the dead were carried away for burial, all efforts went to putting out the fires so that the salvage work could begin. In spite of everyone's efforts, the *Arizona* burned for three and a half days. Even after its fires were extinguished, the metal was too hot to touch. A week later, salvage efforts began, but there was not much to save. Between 1942 and 1943, divers made several exploratory ventures to inspect the ship, but the possibility of restoring the *Arizona* to service was finally dismissed.

During the course of those dives, however, a number of items were recovered. Several safes, including the post office safe, were salvaged. Large amounts of china and silverware were recovered from the officers' messes. Even chairs from the ship's barbershop were saved and reconfigured to make machine gun stands. Two of the ship's anchors were also brought to the surface. Later, the ship's aft turrets were removed and positioned at Army installations on the island for use in case of an invasion.

One of the most difficult salvage efforts was the *Oklahoma*. The *Oklahoma* had taken five torpedo hits in rapid succession, listed, then capsized, trapping a number of sailors inside. I had gotten a glimpse of it from where I was inside the director on the *Arizona*, seeing the battleship roll over. It was hard to imagine such a huge ship turning over like that. It looked like a harpooned whale slowly baring its underside. As she started to capsize, two more torpedoes hit her, making it a total of nine torpedoes that had struck her. Then, while her men were abandoning ship, several Japanese Zeros strafed them.

Many of the *Oklahoma* sailors who were trapped inside died, but incredibly, a number of them survived the torpedoes and the inrushing water. Crews worked around the clock to free them, using everything from cutting torches to crowbars. The next day, eleven men were rescued from one pocket in the hull, and thirteen were freed from another. Righting the *Oklahoma* was an engineering marvel of epic proportions, but, with the help of an innovative private contractor, they did it.

A gunner's mate on the *Oklahoma* described the mood of all the men, observing there was "a deep, powerful thirst for revenge on the part of every enlisted man." Contrary to what you might think after the destruction of so much of their fleet and the deaths of so many of their men, morale was high. The sailors, in fact, threw themselves into the salvage efforts, working long hours and often in dangerous circumstances, determined to get their ships patched up and back in the fight as soon as possible.

ON THE HOME front, a surge of patriotism filled the country with resolve. By Sunday evening, after news of the attack was broadcast on radios across the country, phones rang off the hook at the various recruiting stations. The next morning the naval recruiting office in Washington, D.C., which usually had only three applicants on an average morning, had two hundred young men show up, eager to enlist. By December 11, the date Congress declared war on Japan's Axis allies—Nazi Germany and fascist Italy—the great majority of the country's young men were elbowing for a place at the front.

In Birmingham, Alabama, six hundred men showed up to volunteer in just a few short hours. However, officials estimated that 450 of them would have to be sent home, because they were either too young, too old, or couldn't pass the physical. Even veterans from World War I came to enlist. Offices for the armed services opened twenty-four hours a day, seven days a week, often having lines that stretched around the block.

Boston Red Sox legend Ted Williams was one of the first athletes who stepped up to the plate to enlist. He was followed by a long list of other athletes from all backgrounds, including Jewish Detroit Tigers star Hank Greenberg and African-American heavyweight champ Joe Louis.

Hollywood talent appeared on the radio, encouraging everyone to buy war bonds. Rita Hayworth was one of them, and I have to tell you, that didn't hurt morale. And there were others, Bob Hope and John Wayne, to name a couple. Their leadership inspired everyone. In Texas, for example, the senior class of Baird High School forwent its class picnic and used the

$37.50 allotted for the picnic to buy bonds. The entire nation volunteered in some way or another, from Boy Scout troops that collected scrap metal to grandmothers who knit woolen socks. Farmers and factory workers did their part, too.

The Department of Agriculture urged farmers to plant crops "fencepost to fencepost" in order to feed our Army and Navy overseas. Sugar was rationed. Butter, too. And textiles such as wool and cotton soon became scarce. So did leather, rubber, and most metals, including copper, tin, zinc, and lead. Chrome would also be in short supply; Americans started taking off the bumpers from their cars and donating them to the war effort.

The War Department required its workers to work as many additional hours as necessary to complete each day's task. And production schedules were expanded to operate factories 24/7. Many private corporations shifted their output to wartime production. General Motors, for example, dedicated all its plants to the war effort.

All the great singers of the 1940s, from Dinah Shore to the Andrews Sisters, also contributed in their own way. So did the big-band leaders, from Glenn Miller to the Dorsey Brothers. Dancers from Gene Kelly to Ginger Rogers threw themselves into the job, as did celebrities, sports stars, and musical talents like Irving Berlin.

Berlin was the beloved composer who gave us "Alexander's Ragtime Band," "Easter Parade," "White Christmas,"

"God Bless America," and literally a thousand other songs. And to the war effort he introduced the song "Arms for the Love of America."

Arms for the love of America!
They speak in a foreign land, with weapons in every hand
Whatever they try, we've gotta reply
In language that they understand.

The lyrics and music to that song were written at the request of Lieutenant Colonel John B. Bellinger, who asked the composer to write something that would communicate to all Americans the need to increase the production of arms and at the same time serve as an inspiration for those in the defense industries. Berlin agreed, stipulating that the profits of the song be given to Army charitable and relief efforts.

The greatest rallier of them all, though, was not a composer or a celebrity, it was a commander in chief. In his wartime fireside chats he brought the country together and he kept it united. Just a day after his speech to Congress, President Roosevelt told the American people the contribution each of them would have to make in order to win the war:

We are all in this war. We are all in it—all the way. Every single man, woman, and child is a partner in the most tremendous undertaking in our American history. . . .

On the road ahead there lies hard work—grueling work, day and night, every hour and every minute.

I was about to add that ahead there lies sacrifice for all of us.

But it is not correct to use that word. The United States does not consider it a sacrifice to do all one can, to give one's best to our nation, when the nation is fighting for its existence and its future life.

It is not a sacrifice for any man, old or young, to be in the Army or the Navy of the United States. Rather it is a privilege.

It is not a sacrifice for the industrialist or the wage-earner, the farmer or the shopkeeper, the tradesman or the doctor, to pay more taxes, to buy more bonds, to forgo extra profits, to work longer or harder at the task for which he is best fitted. Rather it is a privilege.

It is not a sacrifice to do without many things to which we are accustomed if the national defense calls for doing without. . . .

There will be a clear and definite shortage of metals of many kinds for civilian use, for the very good reason that in our increased program we shall need for war purposes more than half of that portion of the principal metals which during the past year have gone into articles for civilian use. . . .

We are now in the midst of a war, not for conquest, not for vengeance, but for a world in which this nation, and all that this nation represents, will be safe for our children. . . .

We are going to win this war and we are going to win the peace that follows. . . .

The American people rose to the occasion, ready to fight. What Japan had done at Pearl Harbor was despicable in the eyes of every American. The Japanese had violated every code of honor that had been ingrained in us since childhood. Since *my* childhood, anyway. You didn't sneak up on someone and hit him in the back of the head, without warning. We called that a sucker punch, and no self-respecting kid did it. If you had a quarrel with someone, you squared off, the two of you, and you duked it out. You fought with your fists, and you fought fairly. And you never kicked him while he was down, either. You let him get up and defend himself.

What Japan did in violating our code of honor riled an entire nation.

When we got up from being slammed to the ground from behind, it was not to square off with the Japanese but to give them a whipping they would never forget.

Nebraska, 1922: A future sailor, born to the vast American Midwest.

The class of 1940: We had survived the Depression, stuck it out on the Great Plains through the Dust Bowl, and would soon meet the challenge of World War II. My image is circled.

A June 1940 U.S. Navy recruiting poster. *Naval History and Heritage Command*

Fresh recruit, 1940.

TOP: My ship: The USS *Arizona* at sea. *National Park Service/USS* Arizona *Memorial Photo Collection*

BOTTOM: The *Arizona* in Puget Sound on January 18, 1941, a few months after I came aboard. According to National Park Service historians, "this is the last close-up view of the ship prior to its loss at Pearl Harbor." *NPS/USS* Arizona *Memorial Photo Collection*

TOP: Gallant men: The crew of the *Arizona*, fronted by its famous band.

BOTTOM: A typically idyllic scene, circa 1940, of nearby Waikiki Beach, Oahu, a popular destination for Pearl Harbor sailors on shore leave. Diamond Head is seen in the distance.
NPS/USS Arizona *Memorial Photo Collection*

TOP LEFT: Captain Mitsuo Fuchida personally led the first wave of planes in Japan's attack on Pearl Harbor. TOP RIGHT: Japanese Zeros on the flight deck of the carrier *Akagi*, December 7, 1941. *NPS/USS* Arizona *Memorial Photo Collection*

BOTTOM: This photo, taken from a Japanese aircraft, captures the opening sequence of the attack on Pearl Harbor, during which the USS *Oklahoma* suffers a direct hit from a torpedo on the far side of Ford Island. The *Arizona* is two rows to the left, paired with the smaller *Vestal*. *NPS/USS* Arizona *Memorial Photo Collection*

A view of Battleship Row taken from a Japanese bomber at 10,000 feet: The *Arizona* is second from the top and has just been struck. *NPS/ USS* Arizona *Memorial Photo Collection*

When the attack started, I ran to my battle station, directing the *Arizona*'s five port-side antiaircraft guns. Unfortunately, Japan's high-altitude bombers were too high for our shells; their fighters and dive bombers were too quick and flew too low. The small burst of dark smoke you see in this picture are our AA-ordinance (along with those of other ships and positions) exploding desperately but futilely above the devastation unfolding in the harbor below. *NPS/USS* Arizona *Memorial Photo Collection*

8:06 A.M.: An enemy's armor-piercing bomb strikes the *Arizona*, detonating the ship's forward magazine. The fireball you see in this photo engulfed my battle station and killed more than a thousand of my shipmates.

TOP: After the fatal explosion, thick smoke ascends from the *Arizona*. My battle station at the port-side antiaircraft director is circled. *NPS/USS* Arizona *Memorial Photo Collection*

BOTTOM: The *Arizona*, with its crippled foremast. Again, my battle station is circled. *NPS/USS* Arizona *Memorial Photo Collection*

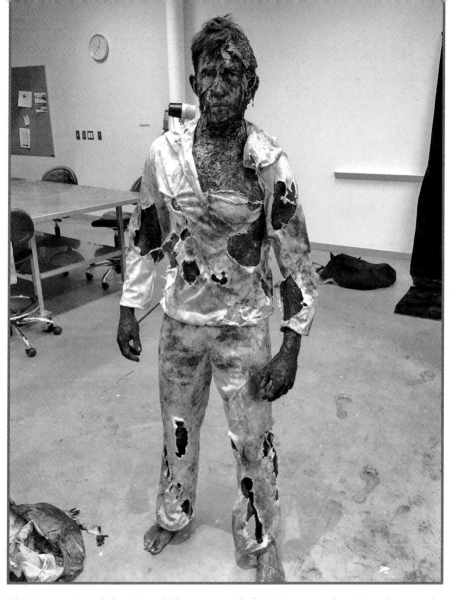

This is approximately how I would have appeared after being rescued on December 7, 1941. Burns covered two thirds of my body. In 2016, the artist Cassidy Newkirk consulted with me to re-create my injuries and appearance on a live model, who posed in makeup for a large-format painting Newkirk is creating of the *Arizona*'s sinking.

The December 8, 1941, issue of the *New York Times*. It was obvious the events at Pearl Harbor would forever change the course of American history, drawing us into the greatest armed conflict the world had ever seen.

BELOW: "A date which will live in infamy"—Franklin D. Roosevelt addresses Congress, December 8. *NPS/ USS* Arizona *Memorial Photo Collection*

LEFT: Oahu, December 8: Marines bury their dead in the shadow of Diamond Point. I was in a military hospital on the island fighting for my life. *Naval History and Heritage Command*

The U.S. Navy's letter to my parents back home in Nebraska: "Your son, Donald Gay Stratton, suffered second and third degree burns on his arms, legs and back, in the recent disaster at Pearl Harbor."

In reply address not the signer of this letter, but Bureau of Navigation, Navy Department, Washington, D. C.
Refer to No. Nav-54-GP
316 69 70

NAVY DEPARTMENT

BUREAU OF NAVIGATION

WASHINGTON, D.C.

January 5, 1942

Subject: STRATTON, Donald Gay,
            Seaman 2d class, U.S. Navy.

My dear Mr. Stratton:

At this date you have undoubtedly been advised by the Medical Officer in Command at the Naval Hospital, Mare Island, California, that your son, Donald Gay Stratton, suffered second and third degree burns on his arms, legs and back, in the recent disaster at Pearl Harbor, and has been transferred to that hospital for treatment.

In all probability your son has communicated directly with you and has kept you informed as to his progress. Further inquiry as to his condition may be obtained from the authorities of that hospital.

The Bureau wishes to assure you of its sincere sympathy in your great anxiety and trusts that your son will experience a speedy recovery.

Sincerely yours,

RANDALL JACOBS
Chief of Bureau

C. B. Hatch
By direction

Mr. Robert Gay Stratton,
Red Cloud, Nebraska.

A pair of snapshots from my stay at the hospital in Mare Island, California. At one point, my weight had dropped from 170 pounds to just 92 pounds.

A Pearl Harbor Veteran at 20, Youth Is Ready to Fight Again

RED CLOUD—Put back in fighting trim by the navy's surgeons, Don Stratton of Red Cloud, veteran of Pearl Harbor, is "ready to go again," as soon as he can re-enlist. The 20-year-old youth, son of Mr. and Mrs. R. G. Stratton, is at his parents' home here after six months in the navy hospital at Mare Island where he received treatment for extensive burns.

Stationed on the ill-fated battleship Arizona when the Japanese struck at Pearl Harbor December 7, Stratton, a first class seaman, was below eating chow when the first bombs hurtled downward on his ship. He ran to his control tower and in the ensuing battle was badly burned over the body and hands, and one ear was partly burned off. He stayed with his ship until it went down in the harbor, blazing. Despite the condition of his hands, burned virtually to the bone, he swung hand over hand by rope to the deck of another vessel which had come up alongside the Arizona to take off its crew.

Stratton came to the United States last December 25 and was sent to the Mare Island hospital

Photo by J. C. Moler, Red Cloud
Don Stratton . . . burned in battle of Pearl Harbor and who is ready to take another crack at the Japs.

"Ready to go again": A local Nebraska news clipping profiling my decision to reenlist in the Navy.

My new ship: In early 1943 I was assigned to the destroyer USS *Stack*, serving as a gunner's mate. The *Stack* arrived at the Pacific front during the Soloman Islands Campaign, and we would go on to participate in the naval battles for the Philippines (including Leyte Gulf, Lingayen Gulf, and Luzon), New Guinea, and Okinawa. *Ray Benoit/Navsource.org*

January 1945: Anti-aircraft fire during the Invasion of Lingayen Gulf. Twenty-four Allied ships were destroyed in this little-remembered but fiercely fought naval battle. *Naval History and Heritage Command*

The Okinawa invasion, April 1945. The *Stack* was present for "L-Day" and is likely one of the ships in the distance. After the war, the *Stack* (sans crew) would survive the atomic tests at Bikini Atoll, before being decommissioned in August 1946. *Naval History and Heritage Command*

Velma, the love of my life, and me on our wedding day, 1950. We have experienced our own tragedies, including the loss of three children, but we've walked together hand in hand through life for sixty-six wonderful years (and counting!).

Still in love: Velma (now ninety) and I (ninety-four) pose in front of our home in Colorado Springs during the writing of this book. If you see the flag raised, you'll know I'm home.

Peter Hubbard

My friend and fellow survivor John Anderson and me at the USS *Arizona* Memorial wall, remembering those we lost. John passed away at age ninety-eight in November 2015. *NPS/ USS* Arizona *Memorial Photo Collection*

LEFT: Gallant men, always: Pearl Harbor survivors gather on a recent December 7 to honor and remember. *NPS/USS* Arizona *Memorial Photo Collection*

BELOW: The USS *Arizona* Memorial straddles the submerged remains of the once mighty battleship that lie where it sunk seventy-five years ago. *NPS/USS* Arizona *Memorial Photo Collection*

ABOVE: A National Park Service diver inspects one of the *Arizona*'s encrusted 14-inch guns. *NPS/Submerged Resource Unit*

Not forgotten: During a ceremony at the memorial, I drop a flower on to the remains of the *Arizona*—the final resting place for 1,102 of my shipmates. *NPS/USS* Arizona *Memorial Photo Collection*

8

Recovery

The Japanese had claimed to have taken Midway in the first days of the Pacific war, but the three-segment coral atoll, little more than a refueling stop in peacetime for amphibious Yankee Clippers en route to Manila, had held off landing attempts and repeated bombardments. At 11:40 P.M. [Christmas Eve], anticipating the holiday on his side of the Date Line, a Midway serviceman at the communications shack, after a long silence from the island, radioed the New York Times *news desk cheerily: "We are still here. Merry Christmas."*

—Stanley Weintraub,
Pearl Harbor Christmas

The days and nights merged together those first few days. I don't remember much with clarity.

Except the maggots!

Using maggots to eat away dead tissue is a medical practice that is centuries old. They even have a name for the procedure: maggot debridement therapy, or MDT for short. I'm not making this up: military surgeons discovered that soldiers who had wounds infested with maggots fared better than soldiers who didn't. The reason? Maggots only feed on dead or diseased tissue, not on live, healthy tissue. The doctors used the procedure only once on me, but it's the kind of thing you tend not to forget.

The other days were fairly routine. Each day the nurses cut away a little more dead skin when they changed my dressings, then they bathed away what had oozed from my wounds during the night, and afterward applied fresh dressings. The pain was terrible. And I could hardly move. Each time I did, it felt as if my skin was cracking.

Later in the month the powers that be decided that patients who needed more than three months of treatment should be transferred stateside. One of the staff came by the ward to find men healthy enough to take a ship back to the West Coast for more specialized treatment at the Naval Hospital on Mare Island, near San Francisco.

"I'll go," I said, straining to raise my hand.

The man looked at me skeptically. "No. I don't think you'd make it. Maybe next time."

"I want to go anyway."

"Fine. If you can stand up and stay up while I change the linens on your bed, then we'll see about it."

I had lost a lot of weight by now, and a lot of strength. I wasn't sure I could do it, but I eased myself off the bed, careful not to let on how painful it was. I pushed myself upright. Put one leg over the side. Then the other. I braced myself with my hands on the bedside, then pushed off. My feet hit the cool floor, and they didn't buckle under the weight. They held me up. Don't ask me how, but they did. I gathered what little reserve I had left and channeled it to my legs. I stood as he changed the sheets. When finished, he wrote something on his clipboard, then looked up, the slightest of smiles on his face.

"We leave the nineteenth."

I thanked him, but I didn't move. I didn't want him to know that I didn't have the strength to get back into bed. When he left, I fell onto the sheets, totally exhausted but totally excited, thinking to myself, *Mare Island. Stateside. I'm going home!*

We weighed anchor late afternoon of December 19. I learned then that ours wasn't the only ship leaving. There were eight or nine others in the convoy. When the ships sailed, many of the women of Hotel Street sailed with them. They aided the nurses on board by changing the bed linens the men had soiled. They helped bathe them, feed them, encourage them, sitting by their bedsides, keeping vigil, cooling their foreheads with washcloths, and keeping them company for the long voyage home.

I later learned that Alvin Dvorak, one of the men who had crossed from the *Arizona* to the *Vestal* with me, was somewhere on that ship going to Mare Island, too. He ran the Sixth Division, making sure everyone got to his battle station. He also commanded the shore boats. He was a nice guy, for all the authority he had. And he was the last man to forehand himself over the rope that tied the two ships together. He had been burned really badly. I didn't see him after that, because he and Bruner were shuttled to the *Solace*, while the rest of us were taken to the inland hospital.

We had taken a northern route to get to the States, since the chances of sailing into the crosshairs of a Japanese periscope were lower that way. The passage across the Pacific was hard, over a lot of rough waters. When a battleship hits swells, its length and width stabilize it in high seas. Smaller ships, like the one I was on, get tossed around a lot. And I felt every wave, each sway of the ship. It was hard on me, partly because of my own pain, of course; but the mood was amplified by the other 124 on board who were fighting their own pain, calling out to God for mercy or to a nurse for morphine.

———————

THE TRIP FROM Hawaii to California took five days.

The closer we got to America, the higher our spirits were lifted. We were told we would arrive Christmas morning. What a present *that* was! The last night, Christmas Eve, our anticipation was so high we almost didn't need the morphine.

We all arrived on the West Coast at eight in the morning, Christmas Day, just as we were told. All, that is, except one, who had died during the night.

Dvorak.

TWO FERRIES WERE waiting to take us to our new home. By the time everyone was loaded onto them it was noon. When the women from Hotel Street asked if they could go with us to the hospital, just to visit awhile and say their goodbyes, the Navy personnel said no, they couldn't. That was the last we ever saw of them. It wasn't right that they were treated so dismissively. To this day I feel bad about that.

When we reached Mare Island, it was late afternoon. The hospital staff welcomed us, wishing us "Merry Christmas." To my eyes, it looked nothing like Christmas, at least the ones I remember in Nebraska. But it was the best holiday ever.

Mare Island is located twenty-five miles northeast of San Francisco, on San Pablo Bay. The compound on the island had been built in 1870 to provide medical services for the naval fleet, but it had gone through several expansions over the years to accommodate sailors from World War I.

It took a while to recuperate from the voyage, and even longer to feel well enough to appreciate the surroundings. The main building was impressive with its stately columns, tall and white, surrounded by neatly manicured grounds. The entire island was a little less than a thousand acres, a perfect place to convalesce. The sight of the rolling landscape, the sound of waves lapping its shores, and the smell of the sea through our open windows all contributed to our healing, almost as if it were a therapy of its own.

I was placed in a ward with two dozen or so other men. A wide corridor ran down the middle of the long room, and a row of beds, placed head to wall, lined each wall. My bed had a canopy over it, since my skin was a hot patch of open sores. To keep me warm, they put a lightbulb in my bed, rigging it to where it wouldn't set the sheets on fire or burn me while I slept.

I became friendly with the men in the beds next to me, but I grew closest to Clarence Dobson, or "Dobby," as he liked to be called. He had served with me on the *Arizona,* but since he was on the other side of the ship, he had been more a passing acquaintance. We both were in pretty bad shape, but we were still able to talk. Neither of us, though, spoke about what happened on December 7. That may seem odd, but we didn't.

Mare Island Hospital was the West Coast center for

neuropsychiatric patients. It was also the regional center for the care of amputees. I didn't know all that was wrong with me, but I knew I didn't want to be in *either* of those groups.

I was a candidate for the neuropsychiatric classification, because if someone touched my skin while I was sleeping, I reacted, sometimes violently, where I'd almost swing a fist. If it hadn't hurt so much to move, I might have actually swung it. Also, I found myself jumping at sharp noises that I wasn't expecting. I had a lot of anger, I could feel it, but I kept it inside. And that made me a candidate, too.

Whichever group I belonged in, though, I knew I had a long row to hoe in front of me. Skin grafts, operations, rehab, plenty of pain, and a lot of just learning to live with what they couldn't fix. I felt like crying, but I didn't. Instead, I prayed. *Looks like I'm going to make it, Lord. Thank you.* And I prayed for the men aboard ship, for the ones who didn't make it.

I remember the Navy chaplains who came, how they talked with me, encouraging me. I also recall the endless parade of strangers who came through our ward, looking for loved ones. I remember how loud they were and how irritated I got with them. *Would they* never *leave?* Maybe it was just my own anger coming out. Or my grief over the sudden loss of connection to the outside world.

Lord, when will all this end?

In the hospital new communities sprang up, however small and short-lived. Nurses, doctors, other patients. I remember the nurses there remarkably well. They were mostly young, mostly misses, but some were career nurses who were older. Miss Jones. Miss Lindquist. Miss Haite. Miss Hanwell. Miss Lee. Miss Thorpe. Miss Aircashay. They all dressed smartly, in naval uniforms. There was also a medic named Frosty. He did a lot of things around the hospital—chores the nurses didn't want to do, like emptying bedpans. I wish I had kept up with them. They were such good people, and they gave so much.

The physician assigned to me was Dr. Hoffman. He did skin grafts, flaying skin from my buttocks, my stomach, and my inner thighs, patching up places where the skin didn't look like it was growing back. He used a small, handheld machine that sliced a layer of skin at a time. Usually someone deadened my skin beforehand, but once I recall—as vividly as I remember the maggots—no one deadened my skin. I don't know why I didn't bring that to the doctor's attention before he operated. And I sure as all get-out don't understand why I didn't bring it to his attention *while* he was operating. But I didn't. Perhaps I had come to accept pain as an ever-present fact of life at the time.

Little by little, I got patched up. It was painful as the skin grew. Some of the scars, though, didn't heal. It seemed everywhere on my body was a hot spot, trying to heal. Because it was so agonizing to move, I didn't, even though the new skin itched something awful. My arms locked into place after they had healed. Because of that, I slept in such a way that caused bedsores to develop on my elbows. The nurses had to keep turning me over so they wouldn't get worse. Dr. Hoffman remedied this by cutting the tendon in my arm and lengthening it.

If I hadn't had Dobby to keep me company, I don't know what I would have done. He had been burned terribly, and we ended up becoming partners in pain. Over that endlessly excruciating year, we became as close as brothers. Eventually, we got to where we could sit up and play cards. Gin mostly, and Hearts. We sometimes played until dark, but the hospital, fearing the Japanese might invade us, was blacked out after the sun went down, cutting short our games.

We both got a lot of saline treatments, where several of the medical team took hold of your sheet, lifting you off the gurney and putting you into a bath of salt water. Initially, they sedated me for those treatments. But they weaned me off the medication fairly quickly. The first few times were hard, but I got used to the treatments, even looked forward to them. In spite of all the work, though, my left side was slow to heal, both my arm and my leg. The arm was worse. The doctor wanted to amputate, but I wouldn't let him. I couldn't.

How many losses can a person take?

No. I put my foot down. I wasn't going to lose anything else.

Enough!

WE TRIED TO follow the war, especially the battles in the Pacific. We got bits and pieces from the nurses and from Frosty. There was a radio in the ward, and a newspaper circulated from bed to bed, so at least we were able to keep up. It didn't look good. The Japanese were running amok through the South Pacific, bombing the daylights out of the Philippines, taking one island after another. They hit the Philippines, I learned, the day after they struck us at Pearl. And the Japanese kept coming at them until they backed our boys into a peninsula on the island of Luzon called Bataan. Many of our soldiers were sick, and many more were starved half to death. After three months of giving all they had, they had nothing left, and they surrendered. Some seventy-five thousand of our men and Filipino soldiers were taken captive.

It was a sad day when we heard the reports of the surrender, and it affected everyone in the ward. Nurses, too. But not all the news was depressing. In late April 1942, we heard about the "Doolittle Raid," a daring strike on Tokyo led by Lieutenant Colonel James Doolittle. "Doolittle's Raiders" brought the fight right to the emperor's doorstep. We found out later that President Roosevelt called his Joint Chiefs of Staff together a couple of weeks after the Japanese hit us, and he told them to come up with a plan to bomb the enemy capital. Tokyo! *Good for you, Mr. President. And good for Doolittle and his Raiders.*

The Japanese leaders had sold their people a bill of goods, claiming they were invulnerable. It was their destiny, and no one could stop them. Well, the Raiders sure gave them something to think about. It was a bold plan. They were to get an aircraft carrier as close as they could, then sixteen B-25s were to take off from its deck. B-25s! No one had ever flown a B-25 off a carrier before. They had to strip them down so they could carry extra fuel. Even so, they didn't have enough to make it back to the carrier. They had worked the numbers, but no matter how they figured, the math was against them. Besides, it was one thing to fly a B-25 off the deck of a carrier; it was another thing to land one. The plan was to bomb Tokyo, then fly to China and hopefully land safely in friendly territory. It came at a cost—every one of those eighty men knew it but still went ahead. Three died during the mission or were never found. The rest ditched their planes over mainland Asia, as planned. Eight were subsequently captured by the Japanese and entered the enemy's notorious prisoner-of-war system; half would not survive the experience. The sixty-nine remaining Raiders successfully made it to friendly territory in China; but they were scattered across the countryside, often in remote regions—facing the daunting task of finding their way home from the other side of the world.

But they did it. And, even knowing that some of them would be captured, tortured, and killed, they would have done it again.

That is the difference between men who are gallant and those who are merely brave.

The gallant would have done it again.

ALTHOUGH THE DOOLITTLE raid was of little tactical advantage in terms of what the bombers destroyed, it was of enormous psychological value. For us at the hospital it was a morale booster that couldn't have come at a better time. And we sent those warlords a clear message: *If we can hit you there, we can hit you anywhere.*

I gained a lot of enthusiasm. We all did. I felt I could take on the challenges ahead of me.

One of those challenges was learning to walk again. Dobby and I had been bedridden so long, on our backs with our feet naturally falling forward, that they fixed in that dropped-down position. And so when we started to walk, we had to throw our feet forward. Added to that, so many of my muscles had atrophied. My legs looked all spindly, like piano legs.

On the morning of December 7, I weighed 170 pounds. Now I tipped the scales at 92. But I was determined to get back on my feet, a day at a time, a step at a time. As I felt around on my body, I noticed I had several numb spots on my legs. I talked to the doctor about them, and he said it would take years to get the feeling back, if then. The scars that healed were tight, and when I made any movement that stretched them, it burned. When I stood up, blood rushed to my legs, setting them on fire. And, boy, did that ever hurt. I walked tentatively. I never fell, not once, but there were some times when I felt I was going to pass out from the pain.

I REMEMBER THE first time I saw my face in the hospital. I had gotten myself out of bed. I was a little dizzy, and so I walked slowly, steadying myself as I went. The mirror was above a washbasin in an adjoining room where the shower was. When I got there, I couldn't believe what I saw. A skeleton stared back at me. My eyes were sunken, and part of my ear was gone, as was a portion of my nose.

I was horrified.

I immediately thought of Mama. The first telegram they received from the Navy said I was missing in action. She was beside herself. When they sent another telegram, saying I was at a hospital on the West Coast, she wanted to come. Papa, too. They had written, wanting to see me, but I knew they didn't have the money to make the trip. I also suspected she would break down when she saw me. I didn't want *that*. So I wrote back, telling them I was okay and that I would rather they not come.

Moving on from sponge baths, I started taking showers. The warm water, though, aggravated my scars. Everything irritated my skin. Still, it felt good to be making progress. Dobby and I used to be fed from trays on our beds, but we eventually got strong enough to walk to the mess hall. Painful as that pilgrimage was, the exercise was good therapy. The social connection helped, too.

Finally the day came when I reached the end of my treatments at Mare Island. I was transferred to a Navy hospital at Corona for rehabilitation.

Corona was outside of Los Angeles. I had heard the hospital there was nice, but it turned out to be a resort, literally: the facility was housed in the old Norconian Hotel. It wasn't new—it had been built in 1923—but it was new to the Navy. In fact, they closed the deal the day after the attack on Pearl Harbor. Little did they realize then, as they were evaluating the purchase, just how much the Navy was going to need it. The staff was all new, most of the doctors coming from the renowned Mayo Clinic in Minnesota. They arrived in April, and we were some of their first patients. By the end of the war, though, there would be five thousand sailors recovering there.

It sat on seven hundred lush acres with a scenic view of the mountains behind it and a serene lake in front. It had 250 luxurious bedrooms, a theater, a ballroom, tennis courts, a golf course, an Olympic-sized pool, elaborate wrought-iron gates, art deco throughout, majestic pillars, marble floors, lavish murals. It was the place where movie stars came when they wanted to get away from show business.

How in the world did the Navy ever afford this? I wondered.

When the Depression hit, it hadn't only affected rural farms; it also affected luxurious resorts. The drought hit them hard, just like it hit us. Hollywood stars and studio executives still made movies, but they no longer got the salaries they once did, and they stopped coming to the Norconian. It closed in 1933. It was reopened in 1935, and it looked like it was going to make a comeback. Walt Disney threw an extravagant party there in 1938, after the studio finished *Snow White and the Seven Dwarfes,* but it just cost too much to keep up the place, and its owners were forced to close its doors. My guess is that the Navy bought it for a song, though the exact price is still debated.

WHILE AT CORONA we learned of the Battle of Midway, waged from June 4 to 7, 1942. What a way to begin the summer. It was all over the radio, no matter what station you turned to.

Admiral Isoroku Yamamoto, leader of the Japanese navy,

became convinced that the U.S. Pacific Fleet was thwarting Japan's imperialist goals in the South Pacific. They had to break the fleet's back, and they would do that by destroying the aircraft carriers that had eluded them at Pearl Harbor.

Midway was a small U.S. naval base halfway between Hawaii and Japan, hardly significant for Japan strategically. But the admiral's ploy in attacking it was to lure the U.S. fleet to come to its defense. Yamamoto had gathered almost his entire naval force for the attack: 6 aircraft carriers, 11 battleships, 13 cruisers, 45 destroyers, along with a number of submarines, transports, and minesweepers. In dividing his force into five fighting units, Yamamoto planned to overwhelm the United States, taking us by surprise, then finish the work he had left unfinished at Pearl Harbor.

Unfortunately for Yamamoto, Navy cryptanalysts had cracked the Japanese code shortly after the war began. Tipped off, Admiral Raymond Spruance devised a counterstrategy. He stationed two attack fleets two hundred miles northeast of Midway. Early the morning of June 4, when the Japanese launched their attack, one of our scouting planes in that area found their fleet.

Our planes took off, and they caught the fleet at a vulnerable time with its carriers refueling and aircraft rearming. Fifty of our torpedo bombers dropped to sea level, skimming the surface, and came in for the kill. Japanese fighters swooped down on them, destroying all but six of the forty-one planes.

But while their pilots were focused on those gallant torpedo bombers, they had left their own fleet unprotected. Everyone's attention was on the battle at sea level. No one bothered to look up. If they had, the Japanese would have seen our dive bombers falling from the skies. Within minutes, three of their carriers were ablaze.

By the end of the battle, the United States had lost 1 carrier, 1 destroyer, 145 aircraft, and had suffered around 300 casualties. The Japanese, on the other hand, lost 4 of their 6 carriers, 1 cruiser, and 292 aircraft; they suffered 2,500 casualties.

As a result of that battle, the balance of power in the Pacific shifted. Midway was the turning point. Spirits couldn't be higher. Only six months had passed since the Japanese decimated the U.S. fleet at Pearl Harbor, and now we had a victory of our own.

BECAUSE THE HOSPITAL staff had arrived only a short time before the first batch of sailors, they didn't have a lot of things in place. There wasn't much urgency, because it was a rehab facility, for the most part. Nobody's life hung in the balance. We were monitored, but we had plenty of time to ourselves to rest and rehabilitate. You could walk around the grounds, swim, lift weights, whatever you wanted. It was a nice summer, but when it was over, I was itching to leave. I wanted my life to get back to normal, wherever *that* was. Though I didn't know where normal was, I knew it wasn't here, lounging around the Norconian. A man can take only so much rest, and then he has to get back to work.

While waiting for my discharge to be processed, I said my goodbyes to the staff and some of the patients.

I got my walking papers in September 1942, with a "Medical Discharge" from the military. No matter what adjective you put before the word *discharge*, it still means you are out of the Navy.

I learned real quick what that meant: when they say you're out, you're *out*.

And though I was going home, I had to find my own way to get there.

9

Home to Red Cloud

He never had the sense of home so much as when he felt he was going there. It was only when he got there that his home-lessness began.

—Thomas Wolfe, *You Can't Go Home Again*

The title of Thomas Wolfe's 1940 masterpiece came from a conversation he had with friend and fellow writer, Ella Winter, who remarked to him: "Don't you know you can't go home again?" Wolfe loved this line so much that he asked permission to use it as the title of the book he was writing. At the end of the novel, he repeats those same words in a moment of reflection by his main character. "You can't go back home to your family, back home to your childhood . . .

back home to a young man's dreams of glory and of pain . . .
back home to places in the country, back home to the old
forms and systems of things which once seemed everlasting
but which are changing all the time—back home to the es-
capes of Time and Memory."

I had a good feeling about going home, and I was really
looking forward to it.

I could walk pretty well by now. And I didn't look like
Frankenstein anymore. I had put on some weight. I wasn't
skin and bones, but I wasn't back to where I was when my
folks last saw me, either. Still, I felt I had the strength to go
home and see my family.

I just wasn't sure if *they* had the strength to see me.

I had to hitchhike home. When I got to Anaheim in Southern California, I looked up an old buddy of mine, Bud Reyn-
olds, who had graduated with me from high school. I thought
he might like to go home for a visit. The two of us had gotten as far as Kansas when he decided he needed to get back
to Anaheim. I caught a ride north with a man who drove
a tanker for Peterson Oil. I still remember his name: Buck
Bartley. Red Cloud was on his way, he said. And that is how
I made my way home.

On the road into town we passed some quaint old buildings. Never gave them a second look when I lived here, but
now they were as captivating to me as ancient monuments.

Red Cloud didn't have a town square, just one long street

running through it with buildings on either side. That's where I was dropped off. On that long street through the middle of town. With buildings on either side where neighbors did their trading and tacked flyers onto creosote-coated poles for those looking for work or needing work done.

I stood on the sidewalk in my white naval uniform with my bag in tow. Just stood. Looking. Things must've picked up since the war. Half the stores were shut down when I left, boarded up and left derelict. Most of those stores now had a new owner, a new front, and, from the looks of it, a lot of business.

The town marshal drove by, stopped when he saw me, backed up, and offered me a lift. The marshal gave his condolences about my ship and my shipmates, thanked me for the sacrifices I had made, for my service to the country. I nodded, not quite sure what to say. I never liked attention, felt uncomfortable being the center of things. I got a little of that in sports, but people mostly said things like, "Good game against Bladen, Donny," or whoever we had played that week. That's different. Pretty much all that's expected of you is a thank-you and that's it.

As he talked, I just looked out the window, seeing what all had changed, what hadn't. The barbershop was still open. The Opera House, still closed.

My family lived on the outskirts of town, near where Pop worked. Home had changed since the last time I was there.

The house my folks now lived in was made of white wooden slats with a porch in front and round back. A windmill stood on the property, a lanky, creaky thing, looking held together by baling wire. But the cattle tank under it was full, so it did its job, all that mattered. In our old home I used to be the one to have to pump our water from the ground and carry it, bucket after bucket, to wherever we needed it.

The windmill brought a smile.

Both parents were home, sitting on the front porch when the marshal drove up, inciting a riot of chickens. My folks stood when they saw me, at a loss for words, then teared up. So did my brothers and sister. I didn't cry, but I did drop my bag and hug them. The embrace hurt, but I tried not to show it. At the same time, it felt good. It had been a long time since I hugged anyone, or anyone hugged me.

I didn't know if I had forgotten how to talk to my family, or if my family had forgotten how to talk to me. Maybe they were afraid to ask about that day, seeing my scars and all.

Mama asked about the hospital, how I was treated. "Did they feed you right?" I had lost a lot of weight in the hospital, and maybe that is what brought Mama's tears. She felt my ribs and said supper would be ready soon, and that lightened everyone's mood. My brother picked up my bag, and the rest of the family hung on me as we walked up the steps of the porch and went inside.

The slap of the screen door behind us and the high-pitched

whine of the hinges caught my ear. I had forgotten the sound of home. The new place was a farmhouse with three bedrooms, a living room, kitchen, and a porch. That was about it. We had all hoped for a bathroom, but indoor plumbing didn't come with the house. Neither did electricity. We had a good time at the supper table, catching up. A lot of boys in Red Cloud had gone off to fight. All the ones I grew up with, in fact.

A number of them weren't coming home, I was told. Bill Shannon had died on the *Arizona*, Pop said. He was three or four years older than me, and so I didn't really know him from school, and he had been in a different division than mine, and so I didn't see him much aboard ship. Still, he was one of our own. And it saddened me to hear the news. And Vencil Sidlo—did I remember him? Mama asked. His dad had a tavern on the north end of town. Been married just a short while before he got called up. Served on a tanker, the USS *Neches* Pop added, but it was torpedoed in January and sank. Fifty-seven men went down with her, including Vencil.

The town had been pretty much devastated, said Mama. She didn't think it could stand one more telegram. It was too much. When they got the telegram saying that I had survived, she went on, she went running across the street to her brother's house, yelling out for the whole neighborhood to hear, "He's alive! He's alive!" The words caught in her throat. She took a napkin and at first just blotted a tear, but then she broke down and cried her eyes out. Between cries she told me how much she had prayed for me, she and all the women at the Methodist church, how they all prayed.

Pop changed the subject and asked about my plans. I was home to stay, I told him, and that pleased them all, putting grins on my brothers and sister.

Pop had a tavern on the south side of town. It was a bar that he had worked at for some time, and when the owner died, he took it over. It was a deep and tall place, with a basement, a bar, some booths, and a few pool tables. He said I could work there, if I liked. But I wanted to see what else was available first. I checked into a few jobs, but there wasn't anything full-time.

The next day I walked down North Webster to the post office to mail a letter. When I went inside, I was surprised to see three murals on the walls. They were painted with tempura by an artist named Archie Musicks, the clerk told me. He finished them in 1941, compliments of the New Deal. Two were in front of the post office as you walked in; the other was to the left over the door. One was called *Loading Cattle*. Another was *Stockade Building*. And the third was *Moving Westward*.

Some things do *change,* I thought to myself, *even in Red Cloud.*

Later I walked to Main Street to get a haircut. Bill Hensman, the barber, was glad to see me, and he wiped his hand

and extended it for a shake. He heard I was coming home, he said. And heard about what happened to me. News travels fast in a small town. He thanked me, and the other men did, too. When Bill finished with the man in his chair, he whisked off the clippings for the next one in line, but he deferred to me. So did the other man in the shop.

Bill's barber chair was one of those good old-fashioned porcelain and polished-metal ones that swiveled. The seat on the high-backed chair was leather, well worn by three generations of Nebraskans. Behind it was a mirror that had seen better days. Overhead were ceiling fans, their wooden slats set on a slow twirl, enough to cool your forehead but not enough to tousle your hair. A potbelly stove sat midway into the long room, but it would be a month before old Bill stoked it up again.

Bill had an old Philco radio, always turned on. Usually the dial was set on music, but not this time. I remember it was broadcasting a farm report, talking about how much a bushel of corn was going for, the price of pork bellies, things like that. The markets were all up, and everyone in Red Cloud was up with them, feeling the local economy was heading down the right road with the ravages of the Depression getting smaller in our rearview mirror. It was beginning to feel like home again. Bill was a talker, and we discussed the war. When he finished, he dusted me off and said, "This one's on me. Thanks for what you done, Donny." I nodded, thanked him. "Good to have you back," said one of them, and the others echoed the sentiment.

"Good to *be* back."

AFTER A LOT of dead ends, I ended up working for Pop, tending bar. It was a long bar, and he took one end while I covered the other. The patrons talked a lot about the war. For all the advice they had, you'd have thought they were the president's cabinet.

As for me, my wounds were getting better, and every day I felt a little stronger. My legs still bothered me, though, and they often burned all to hell. My left side felt a little gimpy, my arm and my leg. It wasn't noticeable to others, but *I* could tell.

After a while, I took a job working for one of my dad's distributors, driving a truck in Hastings, dropping off empty kegs and taking back the empties. The kegs were aluminum and held twenty gallons of beer. They weighed 175 pounds each when full, and I wheeled them into bars on a large dolly that carried two kegs. After that I worked for DeMars Distributing Company, doing pretty much the same thing.

Little by little my arms were bulking back to what they used to be. So were the muscles in my legs, my lower back, my upper body. The hard work was good for me, in more ways than just the physical part of it. After so long lying in a bed, it was a blessing to get out, to be around people who had normal lives instead of being surrounded by all the pain I'd witnessed at the hospitals.

On my day off, I went to the picture show. I settled into a seat in the theater and watched the newsreels showing the most recent footage of the war. Part of the reel showed the war in Europe; the other, the Pacific. I squinted to see if I recognized any of the men in sailors' uniforms. I didn't. But seeing the ships in open waters made me long to be at sea.

It wasn't long before I realized I didn't belong in Red Cloud. My place was in the Navy. I wanted to go back. *Needed* to, perhaps. Partly out of revenge, I'm not ashamed to say. Mostly, though, I think, for my shipmates. They were in the harbor, and I was here. They were at their posts, and I was . . .

What was I doing here?

It was so hard being here. Some things were just like they were when I left. Other things . . . I don't know . . .

I just wished things could go back to the way they were. Before that day. Before someone in the sky looked down his sight and said "Bombs away" in Japanese and blew your ship and everyone in it to kingdom come. Before that. Before the smoke and the fire and the eerie *whoosh* that found everything innocent and trusting and carefree . . . and sucked it all right out of me.

PART THREE

10

Back in the Fight

From this day to the ending of the world,
But we in it shall be remembered—
We few, we happy few, we band of brothers.
                    —William Shakespeare

Combat binds you to your brothers-in-arms in a way nothing else can. That is the closeness I felt with the shipmates I lost. And it's also how I felt about the shipmates who were still alive, taking the fight to the Japanese. They were in the South Pacific, and I was in Red Cloud. It didn't feel right. As I said, I wanted to go back. *Needed* to go back.

After over a year at home, I began talking with my parents about reenlisting. They felt that if it was what I wanted to do, they were behind my decision. And so, on February 26, 1944, I went to the draft board in Omaha. I got some resistance at first. They looked at me with suspicion, first eyeing my scars, then examining my discharge papers. And when they heard my story about narrowly escaping death on the Arizona, well, they couldn't make head nor tails of why I was back in front of them seeking to reenlist. I had dodged a pretty big bullet, after all. I had been darn fortunate. So why in the world would I want to press my luck?

Added to those legitimate concerns, they weren't sure I could handle going back to sea with all its rigors, let alone putting me right in the middle of some of the most heated battles of the war.

I'm not sure what swayed them. Maybe I just wore them down. But they relented. Given all the physical issues I had, though, they wanted to make sure I could handle the work on board ship, and so they said I would have to go through basic training again, just to make sure. I can't say I blamed them. The burns on my body had not completely healed, and my muscles were tight, sometimes restricting my movement. To be honest, I wasn't sure myself if I had the strength to do all the lifting, pulling, and carrying that the job required.

By this time a lot of older men were enlisting, some not in as good shape as I was. In March I was sent to a Navy training camp in Farragut, Idaho. Having gone through this training before, I breezed through some of it. The difficult parts stretched me physically, which is exactly what my body needed. Eventually, I turned in respectable scores. I lagged behind in the long runs at first. But I kept at it. I held pace with the older guys, and, little by little, I started gaining on the younger ones.

Because of my experience at sea and in battle, I rose through the ranks quickly and soon was put in charge of a company. They even gave me my own office. I drilled the men and led them on grinders, the long runs we were required to take each day. The men were curious about my scars. They could see them when I wore short-sleeved shirts and shorts, or when we took showers. They were interested to hear about the attack, partly because it was what got us into the war in the first place. But also, I think, because they wanted to know what they were getting into, what it would be like if *their* ship were attacked.

I got along well with my superiors. They respected me for what I had been through, and even more, I think, because I was signing up for the possibility of facing it all again. They wanted me to stay and "push boots" through the camp, as they put it, but I was determined to return to the Pacific Theater and get back into the action. As I've said, I'm not too proud to admit that part of my motivation was personal revenge. I wasn't going to let the enemy get away with what they had done. Mostly, though, I was doing it for my shipmates, to avenge their deaths. If the roles were reversed, I know that they would do the same for me.

In the summer of 1944 I was sent to Treasure Island, a Navy base between Oakland and San Francisco, where I was assigned to serve on a destroyer named the USS *Stack*. Commissioned in November 1939, the *Stack* had four 38mm guns, two dual 40mm guns, six 20mm guns, six torpedo tubes, and two sets of Y guns, for firing depth charges at submarines, along with two sets of heavy-duty depth charges on the stern of the ship. Destroyers were faster than battleships like the *Arizona*, and their speed was their unique contribution to the fleet. The *Stack* could go 49 knots (about 45 mph), while the *Arizona* could only manage 21 knots, max.

I was elated to be back in the Navy and to be among shipmates again. It felt especially great being back in action, I have to say. I was given the job of gunner's mate responsible for four guns. The job included keeping the guns operational, maintaining them, cleaning them, and positioning the ammunition.

BEFORE WE HEADED out to battle in the Pacific Theater, we sailed to Pearl Harbor, stopping to refuel and resupply. As you can imagine, I had mixed feelings about returning there, unsure how it would hit me. Most on the ship knew I had served on the *Arizona*. They had seen my scars, asked about my experiences.

As we slowly made our way into the harbor, we passed

the *Arizona*. I had not seen it since the morning of the attack. I couldn't believe my eyes. All the superstructure had been cut away—for scrap, no doubt. Where once a great ship was moored, there remained only its ghostly visage, hovering eerily just beneath the water's surface.

Every emotion within me started rising, quietly pooling in my eyes.

Then something happened I wasn't expecting, and I certainly wasn't prepared for. A call came over the public address system, mustering all hands on the fantail. When everyone was there, the captain called out: "Is Stratton here?"

I raised my hand. "Here, sir."

He waved me over. Then, without fanfare of any kind, he presented me with a medal. The Purple Heart. The entire crew applauded. The captain didn't give a speech, and he didn't ask me to give one. He just handed me the medal, and that was it—a simple gesture of respect and recognition.

I was relieved I hadn't been asked to speak—if I had opened my mouth, I doubt I would have been able to control the emotions. Even so, it was an extremely difficult moment for me. It would take me years to find my voice where the *Arizona* was concerned, but that display of unity and honor shown by my shipmates on the *Stack* as we glided past the remains of the *Arizona* was a moment of healing, as much as any hospital treatment had been. Though I may have left Pearl Harbor on a stretcher, I had returned on a destroyer. I had recovered my strength, as had my country. I was ready to meet what was coming—and I was bringing a boatload of reinforcements with me.

AFTER A SHORT stay in Hawaii, we shoved off for the South Pacific under the authority of Admiral William Halsey of the Third Fleet.

We saw action pretty quickly, and a lot of it. We saw action in the Japanese-held territory of New Guinea, just north of Australia, then in Leyte Gulf off the Philippines, and finally, we led the invasion of Okinawa, which is 350 miles south of Japan. Our main task during an invasion was to lead the ships that were transporting men to shore. Then we would set a perimeter, always in sight of shore, and make sure those transports were protected from enemy ships, submarines, and aircraft.

I had an interesting experience the night after we left Guadalcanal. We were part of a convoy, transporting soldiers in the South China Sea, which was a treacherous area because of submarines. In the middle of the night during our crossing, two of us were on watch, our headphones tethering us to the ship with long extension cords. After our nightly ritual of stopping by the bakery and getting a fresh loaf of bread and some butter, my partner and I got a call from a nearby transport ship that a man had fallen overboard. Our ship turned off all its lights so we could see better, and we circled the area, looking for him. Our orders: "If you hear him or see him, we'll pick him up. If not, we have to move on."

Fortunately, my partner and I heard the man calling for help. We signaled the bridge, and the ship turned around, scouring the waters with its searchlight. I spotted him, bobbing on the dark water. When we picked him up, he was stark naked, exhausted, and shivering. Turns out he had gotten seasick and was heaving over the rail of the transport ship so hard that he fell overboard.

Later we learned that our sonar had picked up a lone enemy sub in the area. Being so decisively outnumbered, though, the sub decided not to engage.

The battle of Leyte Gulf was short, lasting only from October 23–26, 1944. But don't let the duration fool you. The Philippine Sea, around the chain of islands where the battle was fought, was a roiling cauldron for those four days. On the morning of the 23rd, that sea held the largest assemblage of ships, in terms of tonnage, the world had ever seen. By the evening of the 26th, Leyte Gulf had taken more tonnage to its murky depths than in any other naval battle in history. The Japanese lost four aircraft carriers, three battleships, six heavy cruisers, four light cruisers, 12 destroyers, one destroyer escort, over 600 planes, and 10,500 sailors and pilots. The Allied forces, on the other hand, lost one light carrier, two escort carriers, two destroyers, one destroyer escort, around 200 planes, and a little more than a thousand men. As a result of this devastating blow, Japan never again launched a major naval offensive.

During this decisive battle, however, the Japanese unveiled a terrifying new tactic, called *kamikaze*. Bill Sloan, in his book, *The Ultimate Battle*, explains its origin:

Before late 1944, few Westerners had ever heard the word "kamikaze," and fewer still knew its original meaning. Translated literally from the Japanese, the term means "Divine Wind," and it owns its revered place in Japanese history and spiritual folklore. Its origin can be traced back to 1281, when Chinese emperor Kublai Khan, son of Mongol conqueror Genghis Khan, dispatched a mighty naval armada to invade and seize Japan's home islands.

No man-made force available to Nippon at the time could possibly have thwarted Khan, whose victory seemed assured until a monstrous typhoon off the Japanese coast destroyed many of his ships and scattered the rest. The people of Japan interpreted the great storm as evidence of heavenly protection and credited their salvation to this Divine Wind.

Six and a half centuries later, in the closing days of World War II, with total defeat closing in around the Japanese military, some of its leaders clung to the belief that history could repeat itself. In a desperate to halt another foreign invasion, they devised a modern version of the Divine Wind—powered not by the gods of nature by thousands of young Japanese zealots eager to sacrifice themselves for the emperor.

The first successful *kamikaze* attack happened on October 25, 1944, at the battle of Leyte Gulf. Japanese pilots had crashed their planes into our ships before, but it was usually a measure of last resort. If the pilot's craft had been hit and was going down, it made perfect sense to try to do the most damage before crashing.

But what we experienced at Leyte was different. The psychological effect that the tactic had on those of us who had a bull's eye on our backs 24-hours a day was unnerving, to say the least. At other times, it was downright demoralizing. You never knew when they were going to strike. At first light. Or last light. Or in the middle of the night. More and more they struck under the cover of darkness. Even though our radar could see them, our gunners could not.

One night during that battle, a *kamikaze* fell from the darkness, hitting one of our ships. The explosion lit up the sky. Then, like moths to a flame, several others appeared from nowhere and crashed their planes into the fire.

The *Stack* was part of the task force that invaded Okinawa on April 1, 1945. Our job, at least initially, was to do mine sweeps of the waters around the island, which took three days. We did this with wooden-hulled planes that went over the water and would drag the mines to the surface, where we would explode them. If we found a mine at night, we would circle it with the ship until morning, when we would blow it to smithereens with a 20mm gun. It was such a treacherous area that we shot at anything floating in the harbor. We did this because sometimes there were Japanese soldiers hiding among the debris, explosive devices strapped to their backs, like suicide bombers, waiting to get close enough to blow a hole in our side.

The invasion of Okinawa was the largest amphibious landing in the Pacific theater. Okinawa was considered strategic real estate due to the five airfields the Japanese had built there. By capturing those fields, the U. S. could launch a relentless assault against mainland Japan. Leading the campaign was a massive Navy flotilla of 1,213 ships, along with 104 ships that played a supportive role. And the joint forces of the Navy, Marines, and the Army participated with a total of 451,866 service men involved in the campaign.

To protect our carriers, other high-value ships, and our fighting forces on the island, the Navy set up a perimeter around the Okinawa archipelago. Along this perimeter were stationed destroyers with state-of-the-art radar and sonar to detect any incoming ships or planes. It was called "picket patrol." Along the perimeter were radar picket stations in the ships, spaced a measured distance from each other, that formed a theoretically impenetrable shield around the island. The USS *Stack* was one of the destroyers assigned to that patrol. In all, 206 ships formed the first line of defense along the picket.

The *kamikaze* dispelled the myth of impenetrability.

The first *kamikaze* pilots flew Zeroes and also Vals, which were high-altitude bombers. By 1945, though, the Japanese realized the strategic necessity of these planes in defending the homeland. Their engineers went to work and came up with a design that fit the mission of the *kamikaze* perfectly. The plane was called an Ōka.

The Ōka was a small, single-seat monoplane that weighed less than 1,000 pounds. It was made mostly of wood, along with some steel. Its light weight allowed it to carry 4,000 pounds of fuel and explosives, 2,500 of which were located in the nose section. It was the first "smart" bomb. But it wasn't guided by computers and GPS co-ordinates. It was flown by a pilot whose mission was to crash it into an Allied ship, inflicting as much damage as possible. Although the Ōka had three, solid-fuel, rocket engines, it was not meant to be flown long distances. Its engines were designed merely to allow its pilot to make any adjustments along its descent. The Ōka was transported underneath a larger bomber. When the bomber came within 25 miles of the target, it would release the craft, and then the pilot would glide the bomb to its target.

Between October 25, 1944 and the end of the war in August of 1945, nearly 4,000 suicide missions had been launched against Allied forces. It became the most feared weapon in the Japanese arsenal. One in seven *kamikazes* were successful in sinking or severely damaging our ships, which was a much better success rate than their other planes had achieved.

Okinawa was 82 days of hell. The strategy of the Japanese was to make the battles in the South Pacific so costly for the Allied Forces that we would give up of the idea of invading their homeland.

The waters off Okinawa were a firestorm of an engagement, with around one hundred of our ships sunk or damaged. I vividly remember one of those engagements. We were on picket patrol, forming a protective fence, so to speak, along a perimeter north of Okinawa, when I first encountered a *kamikaze* attack. A *kamikaze* pilot's sole mission was to crash his plane into one of our ships. If we didn't blow them out of the sky with our antiaircraft guns, they were going to knock us out of the water like toy ducks at a carnival arcade.

It was a desperate strategy by an increasingly desperate enemy. Of course, that's not what comes to mind when the *kamikaze* is in its death dive, its wings whistling toward you. One night, in which the darkess overhead seemed to bristle with suicide bombers, a *kamikaze* bore down straight at us. Straight at me, actually. If he had hit us, I would have died in the explosion. Fortunately, he missed, flying just over us and crashing into the water on the other side of the ship. Some of the picket ships, however, weren't so fortunate. We lost five that night.

Besides sweeping the perimeter waters for mines, the *Stack* pounded the beach with its big guns, softening the area so our soldiers would have a fighting chance. We also would help calm the water for seaplanes to land in. We did this by circling an area, then the seaplanes touched down the calm was created by our wake. After landing, the plane came to the side of our ship, where our crane hooked it and lifted it on board. Okinawa was tough. The enemy had dug in and was determined to fight to the death. Our Marines lost a lot of men on that island. They fought gallantly, all of them—for eighty-two straight days.

Okinawa was the last major battle of the bloodiest war the world had ever seen. (It has been pointed out to me that, by virtue of fighting in both the Pearl Harbor attack and the Okinawa invasion, I can claim a small footnote in history for having served at the opening shots and the final battle of America's Second World War.) The campaign claimed the lives of more than a quarter million people. Of those who died, close to 140,000 were civilians living on the island; 107,539 were Japanese servicemen; and 12,274 were U. S. servicemen. The battle pitted the greatest U. S. naval flotilla ever assembled against the most tenacious of enemies, both in the air and on the ground. In the sky, *kamikaze* pilots flew to their deaths as they ravaged the U. S. fleet. On the land, Japanese soldiers fought to the death rather than surrender.

The radar picket ships took the biggest beating of the U. S. naval ships engaged at Okinawa, all the while protecting the rest of our ships from 1,900 *kamikaze* attacks. Fifteen of the picket ships were sunk; 45 were damaged. Causalties of those serving on those ships were 1,348 dead and 1,586 wounded.

Vice Admiral Richmond K. Turner gave this commendation to those who served on that hazardous perimeter:

> The gallant ships in these stations were at all times, and in a very literal sense, in the first line of defense at OKI-NAWA. Their expert raid reporting and efficient fighter direction made possible the timely interception of enemy aircraft which would otherwise have been able successfully to attack our transport and supply ships in force. The enemy pressed his attacks with fanatical determination and still failed to disrupt our progress, largely because the Radar Pickets were an obstacle he could not overcome. By their steadfast courage and magnificent performance of duty in a nerve wracking job under morale shattering conditions, the crews of the ships and craft of the Radar Picket stations have emblazoned a glorious new chapter in the naval tradition.

————

IT WAS DURING Okinawa that I heard the news: President Roosevelt was dead.

It was hard for me, hearing that. He had been such a part of my life, serving his fourth term when he died. He seemed to always have a steady hand on the wheel, guiding us through the Depression and through most of the war. It's a shame he didn't live long enough to see a weary world turning its swords into plowshares.

The war had taken its toll on the president, and those closest to him were concerned. His health had deteriorated, I later learned, and his face was ashen. He retreated for a couple of weeks to his home in Warm Springs, Georgia, which had a natural hot springs health spa on the property. He loved going. He had dedicated the property to treat children and families who had suffered from polio, as he did, and other paralyzing diseases. He felt at home there. He didn't have to hide his disability; and it was there—surrounded by playful children in the pool and by grateful families on the picnic grounds—that something of his own childhood came back to him. Happier times of his younger days. There was no returning to those times in the White House, no escape from the news, which for four long terms had been mostly bad, and often heartbreaking.

On the afternoon of April 12, 1945, President Roosevelt

was inside, sitting to have his portrait painted. At one o'clock he grew tired and told the artist, "We have only fifteen minutes." Then he said, "I have a terrific headache," and fainted. A doctor on the property was called, and he rushed over to give the president a shot of adrenaline, hoping to revive him. It didn't. Within minutes Roosevelt was dead.

His wife, Eleanor, was there, along with his personal secretary, Grace Tully. Funeral cars later pulled into the compound to take away the body. In the past when he left Warm Springs, patients at the spa, many of whom were children, had lined the street that led to his cottage, all of them waving goodbye. Now the street was lined with Marines. Channeling the grief of the nation, Chief Petty Officer Graham W. Jackson, an African-American man who played an accordion many times for the president, was photographed by Ed Clark with tears running down his face as he stood in front of the group that was taking the body away. He played "Going Home," one of Roosevelt's favorites.

As the procession left, the man changed the tune to "Nearer, My God, to Thee."

FDR's vice president, Harry Truman, became our new commander in chief. But how do you fill shoes like those?

The nation mourned. The funeral gave us pause.

But not the war.

The war stopped for no one.

IN JULY 1945, I was given leave from combat to return state-side in San Diego so I could attend Electrical Hydraulics School. The school educated you in all the electronics necessary to fire the guns on board the *Stack*. Those skills were necessary so I could take on greater responsibilities with the guns themselves.

While I was in San Diego, news began leaking out about some of the atrocities the Japanese had committed—the Rape of Nanking and the Bataan Death March among them. The way they treated our prisoners was worse than even the Nazis. We didn't know the full extent of those atrocities until the war was over, but what we heard was beyond what you thought human beings were capable of doing to one another. The war in Europe had ended in May. The country breathed a sigh of relief. But only a sigh. The war in the Pacific was some of the most intense fighting of the entire war, and who knew how many more young men would be lost before the world's great sadness was over?

11

Endgame

The Japanese warlords are receiving, in their own homeland, the retribution for which they asked when they attacked Pearl Harbor.

—Franklin D. Roosevelt

The above words are excerpted from an undelivered address President Roosevelt was planning to give on Thomas Jefferson's birthday, April 13, the day after Roosevelt died. The president was fully aware of a decision he would soon have to make—whether to invade Japan, costing untold casualties on both sides, or to use the new nuclear weapon that carried the hope of ending the war with far fewer casualties.

As it turned out, the decision fell to Harry Truman. Can

you imagine taking over such a huge job at such a crucial juncture in the history of the world and having to make such a decision?

Controversy continues to surround our use of the atomic bomb on Hiroshima and Nagasaki. For many it is an emotionally charged issue. No one understands the rawness of those emotions more than the men and women who served in World War II. We saw so much. There were things we didn't talk about when we came home. It was just too horrendous to go back to some of the places we had been. For those of us who fought and suffered in the war and who saw the horrors of combat, the end of the war couldn't come soon enough.

If I may, I'd like to put the war's endgame into context, at least as I understand it.

JAPAN WAS A small country with too few of the natural resources necessary for it to become a global power. It needed metal, rubber, lumber. Most of all, though, it needed oil. For years the United States had sold Japan its scrap metal and surplus oil, which it used as the raw materials for its conquest of China.

At first, its expansion into China was overlooked. But as Japan took more territory and as news of its atrocities became more public, the United States was forced to act. Not only did we cut off trade with Japan, but Roosevelt used the

Pacific Fleet to form an embargo so that no other countries could provide it with the resources it needed to attain military dominance over East Asia.

This, more than anything, was what led Japan to go to war with the United States. They felt we were keeping them from fulfilling their destiny. And they thought we had no right to do that.

The consensus among Allied leaders was that Japan would not be defeated until they were invaded. But because of how tenaciously Japanese soldiers had fought for land that was not their homeland, like Iwo Jima and Okinawa, the Allies knew they would defend their own land even more tenaciously. In fact, the propaganda their citizens were fed stated that if 100 million died defending their land, their deaths would be a beautiful tragedy, like "shattered jewels."

The code name for the overall invasion of Japan was Operation Downfall. The first stage of that invasion was coded as Operation Olympic. Target date: November 1, 1945. The commander: General Douglas MacArthur.

Many feared that such an invasion would be ten times more costly in American lives than the invasion of Normandy. Those in the highest positions of leadership were asked to give estimates of U.S. casualties if Operation Olympic were to go into effect. In April 1945, the Joint Chiefs of

Staff approximated that casualties for the U.S. Sixth Army in a ninety-day campaign would be 514,072, including 134,566 dead and missing.

In a letter from General Lauris Norstad to General Curtis LeMay, who was to assume command of the B-29 force on Guam, Norstad gave an estimate of half a million U.S. fatalities.

Commander of the Army Service Forces Lieutenant General Brehon B. Somervell estimated U.S. casualties to be around 720,000 dead and wounded.

Secretary of War Henry Stimson and his staff concluded that conquering Japan with an invasion force would cost the United States 1.7–4 million casualties, of which the fatalities would be anywhere from 400,000 to 800,000. Japan's fatalities were projected to be 10 million.

In a memorandum to President Truman, former president Herbert Hoover estimated that half a million to a million Americans would die if we invaded Japan.

A study done by General MacArthur's staff put the final estimate, after a revision, at 105,000.

The lowest assessment that was tabulated came from Admiral Chester W. Nimitz's staff, which was 49,000 ground troops in the first thirty days and 5,000 casualties at sea.

In sum, the numbers were grim, not only for the United States but for Japan.

———

IN PREPARATION FOR the invasion, the United States started a campaign of firebombing Japan's cities, dropping napalm from B-29s. The first city targeted was Tokyo, in the hope that would shock Japan's leaders into surrendering. It didn't, and sixty-six more cities were subsequently bombed. Even then, Japanese leaders were committed to their insane code of honor, refusing to surrender.

In July, the Manhattan Project—which was the code name for the team of scientists who were given the task of building the atomic bomb—successfully detonated the first nuclear blast in the deserts of New Mexico. By August, the atom bomb was added to America's arsenal of weapons.

On August 6 we dropped the weapon on Hiroshima, home of Japan's Second Army.

President Truman gave the Japanese leaders an ultimatum. They had sixteen hours to surrender. If they didn't, he said, they should "expect a rain of ruin from the air, the like of which has never been seen on earth."

They didn't surrender. Three days after the bomb was dropped on Hiroshima, another was released over Nagasaki. On that same day, the Soviets declared war on Japan and launched an assault that overwhelmed Japanese troops in Manchuria.

Finally, on August 14, Japan announced its surrender.

Responding to criticism, President Truman said: "Nobody is more disturbed over the use of atomic bombs than I am but I was greatly disturbed over the unwarranted attack by the Japanese on Pearl Harbor and their murder of our prisoners of war. The only language they seem to understand is the one we have been using to bombard them."

Irving Berlin's 1941 song proved prophetic:

Arms for the love of America!
They speak in a foreign land, with weapons in every hand
Whatever they try, we've gotta reply
In language that they understand.

Brute force was the native tongue of the Japanese military. It was the language they used when they marched across China, when they attacked Pearl Harbor without warning, when they overran the islands in the South Pacific.

They were deaf to the language of decency, of diplomacy, and of nonviolent measures such as trade restrictions, sanctions, and embargoes. Even when their own cities were being destroyed, when the voices of their own people were raised in pain, anguish, grief, and despair, even then they refused to listen. When finally they were spoken to in a language they understood, only then did they listen.

It is tragic that it took such extreme measures from the United States to conclude Japan's reign of terror.

But we ended it.

And we did so, to use Roosevelt's words, "not for conquest, not for vengeance, but for a world in which this nation, and all that this nation represents, will be safe for our children."

HERE I SHOULD add a postscript for those who think less of America for resorting to such extreme measures. Before releasing the bomb on Hiroshima, U.S. aircraft dropped leaflets that warned of the bombing. *Five million* of them. They dropped them on Hiroshima, Nagasaki, and thirty-three other cities that were potential targets. The leaflet, printed in Japanese, is translated as follows:

> Read this carefully as it may save your life or the life of a relative or friend. In the next few days, some or all of the cities named on the reverse side will be destroyed by American bombs. These cities contain military installations and workshops or factories to produce military goods. We are determined to destroy all of the tools of the military clique which they are using to prolong this useless war. But, unfortunately, bombs have no eyes. So, in accordance with America's humanitarian policies, the American Air Force, which does not wish to injure innocent people, now gives you the warning to evacuate the named cities and save your lives. America is not fighting the Japanese people but is fighting the military clique which has enslaved the Japanese people. The

peace which America will bring will free the people from oppression of the military clique and mean the emergence of a new and better Japan. You can restore peace by demanding new and good leaders who will end the war. We cannot promise that only these cities will be among those attacked but some or all of them will be, so heed this warning and evacuate these cities immediately.

The United States controlled the radio station at Saipan, and from there they broadcast a similar message to the Japanese people. They repeated the warning every fifteen minutes.

Five days after America distributed the leaflets, they dropped the bomb. Hiroshima, as the warning said, was destroyed. Utterly. Ninety percent of the city was demolished, and the loss of life was estimated at 80,000–100,000, with thousands to die later from radiation exposure.

After Hiroshima, we dropped more leaflets, which stated the warning more sternly:

America asks that you take immediate heed of what we say on this leaflet. We are in possession of the most destructive explosive ever devised by man. A single one of our newly developed atom bombs is actually the equivalent in explosive power to what 2,000 of our giant B-29s can carry on a single mission. This awful fact is one for you to ponder and we solemnly assure you it is grimly accurate.

We have just begun to use this weapon against your homeland.

If you still have doubt, make an inquiry as to what happened to Hiroshima when just one atomic bomb fell on that city.

Before using this bomb to destroy every resource of the military by which they are prolonging this useless war, we ask that you now petition the Emperor to end the war. Our president has outlined for you the thirteen consequences of an honorable surrender. We urge that you accept these consequences and begin the work of building a new, better and peace-loving Japan.

You should take steps now to stop military resistance. Otherwise, we shall resolutely employ this bomb and all other superior weapons to promptly and forcefully end the war.

The Japanese did not heed this warning, either. Three days after we dropped the bomb on Hiroshima, we released it on Nagasaki, home of a Mitsubishi torpedo factory. This time only a third of the city was destroyed, with casualties about half those of Hiroshima.

Even if you believe America shouldn't have used the atomic bomb on Japan, you should know that we tried nearly everything, short of an invasion, so we would *not* have to use it. It was a reluctant last resort.

One more thing you should know . . .

None of us at Pearl Harbor got leaflets like that from the Japanese.

IT HAD BEEN a long, hard war. Not just for us. For the entire world. And we were weary, all of us. Even Japan.

Before the bombing, Japan suffered crushing defeats at Iwo Jima and Okinawa. U.S. losses at Iwo were 6,800 killed; Japanese, 19,000. The United States suffered 7,600 fatalities at Okinawa; Japan, a staggering 110,000. The Japanese leaders were like a leg-heavy boxer who had gone fifteen rounds against a superior opponent who had backed them into a corner. As if the punches at Iwo Jima and Okinawa weren't enough, three weeks before Hiroshima we pummeled twenty-five more of their cities. Hiroshima was to be the knockout blow, surely. But after all that punishment, they were still on their feet, refusing to give up.

The Allies had issued the Potsdam Declaration, demanding the unconditional surrender of all the Japanese armed forces. If they did not comply with the Allies' demands, it would mean "the inevitable and utter destruction of the Japanese homeland."

On July 28, Japanese prime minister Kantaro Suzuki informed the press that his government was "paying no attention" to the Allied ultimatum. It was then that President Harry Truman gave the order for the destruction to begin. After the bombing of Hiroshima, only a fraction of the emperor's cabinet favored accepting the terms of the Potsdam Declaration, including redrawing borders, resettlement, and trials for war crimes. On August 8, when the emperor was informed of the bombing of Nagasaki and the Soviet's declaration of war against Japan, he called for a meeting of his cabinet.

The gathering was held shortly before midnight on the 9th. It was held in the air-raid shelter located below the Imperial Library. The emperor's eleven-man cabinet was seated around a large table. When the emperor entered the room, his cabinet rose. He walked with heaviness. His countenance was fallen. As he sat in a straight-backed chair, the others took their seats, too. He asked to hear their arguments and patiently listened as they delivered them.

A heated debate soon sparked. In the end, the prime minister, who so cavalierly dismissed the Allies' ultimatum, now urged the emperor to accept its terms, provided he would be able to remain emperor so he could oversee the transition of rebuilding Japan.

The next day, the emperor relayed the message to Washington. After two days of debate, Hirohito accepted the Allied terms of surrender.

On August 15, the emperor addressed his people over the radio. Unlike President Roosevelt, who had addressed the country periodically, Emperor Hirohito had *never* spoken to his people. As it turned out, his speech was difficult for many to understand, because he spoke in classical Japanese rather than the common language the majority of his people spoke. Still, his message got out.

He never used the words "defeat" or "surrender" in his speech. Instead, he spoke in more positive terms, even reversing the ideology of conquest, which he had so fervently espoused during his reign: "To strive for the common prosperity and happiness of all nations, as well as the security and well-being of our subjects, is the solemn obligation which has been handed down by our imperial ancestors and which lies close to our heart. The enemy has begun to employ a new and most cruel bomb, the power of which to do damage is, indeed, incalculable, taking the toll of many innocent lives. Should we continue to fight, not only would it result in an ultimate collapse and obliteration of the Japanese nation, but also it would lead to the total extinction of human civilization."

It seemed clear the emperor saw our use of the bomb as the deciding factor in his decision not to "continue to fight." And, in what seemed a magnanimous act, he stated: "We have resolved to pave the way for a grand peace for all the generations to come by enduring the unendurable and suffering what is unsufferable."

The speech lasted four and a half minutes. When it was over, the people bowed to his decision. Therein was the peace.

September 2, 1945, a Sunday, was the date chosen for the signing of the documents for Japan's surrender. The ceremony took place at 9 am on deck of the USS *Missouri*, which was anchored in Tokyo Bay. The battleship flew the flags of the United States, Britain, the Soviet Union, and China. Also anchored in the harbor were 258 Allied warships. Admirals Nimitz and Halsey were there, along with Rear Admiral Forrest Sherman and General Douglas MacArthur. Before MacArthur formally accepted Japan's surrender, he made this statement: "It is my earnest hope—indeed the hope of all mankind—that from this solemn occasion a better world shall emerge out of the blood and carnage of the past, a world founded upon faith and understanding, a world dedicated to the dignity of man and the fulfillment of his most cherished wish for freedom, tolerance, and justice."

Foreign Minister Shigemutsu of Japan stepped forward and signed the document of surrender, then representatives from all the Allied powers signed it. As a thousand carrier planes and B-29 bombers flew overhead, MacArthur closed with these words: "Let us pray that peace be now restored to the world and that God will preserve it always."

Thank God in Heaven, it was finally over.

AS THE NEWS of the war's end traveled through the airwaves, across boundaries and datelines, and into the radios of families across the world, there was indeed celebration. But there was also pause for reflection. Like this one by Bing Crosby, broadcast on August 15, 1945: *"What can you say at a time like this? You can't throw your skimmer in the air. That's for* run-of-the-mill holidays. I guess all anybody can do is thank God it's over. . . . Today, though, our deep-down feeling is one of humility."

Speaking over the radio the day after V-J Day, Crosby expressed what many of us were feeling when the war ended. There was a confluence of feelings, really. Jubilation, certainly. Relief, my goodness yes: you have no idea what a relief it was to hear the news. Sadness, like you wouldn't believe. So many of our brothers-in-arms would never come home again.

In his book *The Road to Character,* columnist David Brooks describes hearing that broadcast when it re-aired many years later. "The show mirrored the reaction of the nation at large," he wrote. "There were rapturous celebrations, certainly. Sailors in San Francisco commandeered cable cars and looted liquor stores. The streets of New York's garment district were five inches deep in confetti. But the mood was divided. Joy gave way to solemnity and self-doubt."

I heard the news when I was in Hydraulic School in San Diego. It came over the school's intercom. "Now hear this," the announcement began. And it went on to say that the war was over. I remember giving a good "hurrah!" There wasn't much more to it than that. It felt like everything just lifted from my shoulders.

But my joy soon gave way to solemnity and self-doubt.

There is an inscription on a plaque at Pearl Harbor that says: "Why them and not me?" The words are from Paul H. Backus, an ensign on the USS *Oklahoma*. It is not hard to understand why those words haunted him. His ship was hit by nine torpedoes and capsized, trapping so many of his shipmates. Four hundred twenty-nine of them perished. He survived.

I understand the question. It has haunted me, as well. They were dead, my shipmates on the *Arizona*. And I was alive. Some call it survivor's guilt. I don't know what to label it. And I still don't know how to understand it, how best to deal with it.

I thank the good Lord I survived. But why me and not those who fought beside me?

Me, and not Hollowell, who died that day?

Me, and not Dvorak, who died Christmas Eve on the ship to the States?

Me, and not the twenty-one members of the band, all of whom died in an instant?

Me, and not all the gallant men who died that day?

Why me?

I don't know. You can say it was the providential hand of God that put me in a battle station where I would be shielded from the worst of the flames that day. But then what do you say about the *Oklahoma* ramming into us that one foggy day in October? If it hadn't hit us, none of us would have been at Pearl Harbor during the attack. But then, perhaps some other crew would have been targeted in our place.

It will drive a body crazy, trying to do the math on that one and make the equation balance. All I know is what I learned from my mama. I know the Lord is good. Why *I* was saved from the fire, I will never fully understand. I no longer try to do the math. I wore out too many pencils a long time ago.

Instead, I just say a prayer of thanks for me, who made it.

And a prayer of blessing for those who didn't.

And one for the families they left behind.

It's the best I can do.

I came across a simple quote that has helped me, especially at times when I feel I haven't done enough. Maybe it will help when you feel that way, that you haven't done enough. It's not in the Bible. I don't know who said it. I'm pretty sure, though, it *wasn't* Patton or MacArthur. Here it is:

Do the best you can
With what you've got.
It will be enough.

Whenever I think of my fellow shipmates, the ones who didn't make it off our ship, I always feel I could've done more, *should've* done more, though I don't know what that would be. With what I've got, the best I can do is pray. I'm sure of that. Is it enough? That's the part where I'm not so sure. I hope it is. I pray it is. Honestly, though, I don't know.

But I *am* sure of this: if the good Lord isn't merciful, *none* of us has a prayer.

12

The Lessons of Pearl Harbor

*It is our obligation to the dead—it is our sacred obligation to
their children and to our children—that we must never forget
what we have learned.*

And what we have learned is this.

*There is no such thing as security for any nation—or any
individual—in a world ruled by the principles of gangsterism.*

*There is no such thing as impregnable defense against
powerful aggressors who sneak up in the dark and strike
without warning.*

*We have learned that our ocean-girt hemisphere is not im-
mune from severe attack—that we cannot measure our safety
in terms of miles on any map anymore.*

—President Franklin Roosevelt

In FDR's fireside chat at the beginning of the war, the president offered general lessons that the attack on Pearl Harbor

taught us—principally that we should never take our security for granted. But there are other, more specific lessons that I would like to share. I want to be as objective as I can. Forgive me, though, if from time to time I am not. It's personal with me.

I lost a lot of shipmates, many of them good friends.

I lost a lot physically, too, in terms of the trauma my body went through. The effects of that experience have followed me throughout my life, not to mention the emotional, psychological, and spiritual trauma. I carried most of it inside all these years, which, looking back, I don't think was the best thing. Right or wrong, it was my way of dealing with it.

I lost the trust I had in my leaders, too. It was a blind trust, admittedly. Naïve, certainly. But you have to understand, I lived in a time when we respected our leaders, whether they were our teachers, our doctors, our employers, our pastors, or our politicians. It was ingrained in me. I lost that in the weeks and months and years following Pearl Harbor. So much was brought to light, largely because of the investigations that followed; I just couldn't trust anymore, not the way I did, anyway.

IN ALL, THERE were nine investigations into Pearl Harbor. The government didn't waste any time starting theirs. On December 22, 1941, Supreme Court justice Owen Roberts began hearings in Hawaii. A month later, Justice Roberts submitted his findings to President Roosevelt. Admiral Husband E. Kimmel, commander in chief of the Pacific Fleet, and General Walter Short, commanding general of the Hawaiian Department, were both found to be in "dereliction of duty" and were promptly demoted to lesser ranks and retired.

The buck didn't stop there. As it turned out, there was lots of blame to go around. Each investigation shed a little more light on who was culpable, and fingers have been pointing ever since.

As a Pearl Harbor survivor, I have a responsibility to bear witness. If I don't talk about our failures, I feel I would be in dereliction of my own duty. I couldn't live with that. So here is what I believe went wrong.

1. We Lacked Foresight

We prepared to fight the next war with the weapons that won the last war. To illustrate the point, let me tell you the story of Billy Mitchell.

Mitchell was a brash-talking, barnstorming aviator. His love for aviation can be traced back to Kitty Hawk, North Carolina, where he watched Wilbur and Orville Wright fly the first airplane in 1903. He predicted as early as 1906 that conflicts between countries would be won not by sea power, as they had been in the past, but by airpower.

When the United States entered World War I in April

1917, Lieutenant Colonel Mitchell commanded all American aircraft in France. During the Battle of Saint-Mihiel, he coordinated a force of 1,481 British, French, and Italian planes to support American ground forces. The effort was a resounding success. He returned home in 1919 a hero.

After the war, Mitchell was appointed director of the Air Service and was one of twenty-one men chosen by the president to study the merits of airpower. At this time, the Navy was pushing for federal money to build not only more ships but bigger ones, like Britain's so-called superdreadnoughts. After all, they argued, Britain's naval power had turned their island into an empire. The battleship was the weapon of the future, they asserted with almost evangelistic zeal.

Mitchell vehemently objected. Unable to convince the Navy or the Congress, Mitchell took his argument to the press, boldly stating: "Army planes could sink any battleship afloat. And given permission, I'll prove it."

Newspapers ran the headline. Although the Navy didn't budge, Congress did, granting Mitchell approval for the bombing of captured battleships. During the summer of 1921, Mitchell's bombers sank two mothballed U.S. ships. Not long after that, with the public and press as witnesses, the captured German battleship *Ostfriesland,* thought to be unsinkable, was sunk in minutes by Mitchell's airplanes.

In attendance that day, watching it all, learning from it all, were the Japanese.

The performance only emboldened Mitchell, and he spoke out more brashly than ever. He caused such controversy that his commanders sent him as far away from Washington as they could: Hawaii. While there, he reported that Hawaii was a gravely inadequate place for military defenses.

In 1924, Mitchell went to Europe and then to the Far East to study aviation advances being made abroad. After the trip he remarked: "Japan may end up developing the greatest air-power in the world."

Mitchell continued to berate top authorities in the military, Congress, even the White House. As a result, he soon lost his appointment as deputy chief of the Air Service. He was then demoted and sent to San Antonio, Texas. In September 1925, while in Texas, Mitchell received news of one Navy plane crashing and another one getting lost on its way to Hawaii. In response, he accused the leaders of the Army and Navy with incompetence and negligence so great it bordered on treason.

The remark got Mitchell court-martialed. The following is excerpted from one of the exchanges that occurred during the trial.

Prosecutor: You say that the Hawaiian islands, our base in Pearl Harbor, will fall victim to an air attack? Does your crystal ball reveal by what enemy this attack will be made? By whom? By whom?

Mitchell: The attack will be made by the Japanese.

During the seven-week trial, Mitchell was found guilty of insubordination. Instead of enduring the shame accompanying the verdict, he resigned his commission. He died in 1936.

Tragically, Pearl Harbor proved him right. Ironically, we recognized that immediately, naming the bomber used in the Doolittle Raid after him—the B-25 Mitchell. After the war was over, Congress, by a special act, promoted Mitchell to major general, retroactive to the date of his death, and awarded him the Congressional Medal of Honor.

It's a moot point, I know, but I wonder how different history would have turned out if our leaders had heeded Billy Mitchell's foresight. I wonder how different *my* history would have turned out, and that of every other man in that harbor.

2. We Communicated Poorly

Pearl Harbor historian Gordon Prange hit this nail squarely on the head when he wrote: "Of the more localized American mistakes in 1941, many can be boiled down to a failure to communicate. All along the line there was a failure to supply relevant information to juniors; failure to spell out clearly just what was meant; failure to ensure that directives had been fully understood and complied with; and failure of juniors to be sure they understood their superiors. Above all, there was a failure to understand that possible doubt should always be resolved in favor of clarity."

Here is the context in which those failures of communication occurred. Negotiations with Japanese diplomats in Washington had come to an end in the latter part of 1941 when both countries refused to budge. Japan insisted the United States lift its oil embargo and not interfere with Japanese expansion into East China. We countered, saying the only way we would lift the embargo would be for Japan to pull out of East China and cease all hostilities against it. When this stalemate appeared unresolvable politically, we knew it could only be settled militarily.

In January 1941, Admiral Kimmel and General Short were advised by the secretaries of the Navy and the Army that Japan might launch a surprise attack against the Pacific Fleet at Pearl Harbor. They went on to say the attack would most likely be from the air. Below is the warning General Short received from the War Department, two weeks before the attack.

PRIORITY MESSAGE NO. 472 TO COMMANDING GENERAL, HAWAIIAN DEPARTMENT

Negotiations with Japan appear to be terminated to all practical purposes with only the barest possibilities that the Japanese Government might come back and offer to continue. Japanese future action unpredictable but hostile action possible at any moment. If hostilities cannot, repeat cannot, be avoided the United States desires that Japan commit the first overt act. The policy should not, repeat not, be construed as restricting you to a course of action that might jeopardize your defense. Prior to hostile Japanese action you are directed to undertake such reconnaissance and other measures as you deem necessary but these measures should be carried out so as not, repeat not, to alarm civil population or disclose intent. Report measures taken. Should hostilities occur you will carry out the tasks assigned in Rainbow Five [the Army's basic war plan] so far as they pertain to Japan. Limit dissemination of this highly secret information to minimum essential officers.

MARSHALL

That same day Admiral Kimmel received a similar warning from the Department of the Navy (X indicates a period):

From: Chief of Naval Operations
Action: CINCAF, CINCPAC
Info: CINCLANT, SPENAVO
272337
This dispatch is to be considered a war warning X Negotiations with Japan looking toward stabilization of conditions in the Pacific have ceased and an aggressive move by Japan is expected within the next few days X The number and equipment of Japanese troops and the organization of the naval task forces indicates an amphibious expedition against either the Philippines Thai or Kra Peninsula or possibly Borneo X

Execute an appropriate defense deployment preparatory to carrying out the tasks assigned in WPL 46 [the Navy's basic war plan]. Inform district and army authorities X A similar warning is being sent by War Department X Spenavo inform British X Continental districts Guam Samoa directed to take appropriate measures against sabotage.

General Short had received the warning: "Impending hostile Japanese action." And Admiral Kimmel had been advised, "This dispatch is to be considered a war warning."

The week before the attack, the following messages had been intercepted by our codebreakers:

Destroy all codes; burn secret documents.
Retain only such confidential material as is necessary.

Something is about to happen when you tell your diplomats in Washington to destroy all codes, burn secret documents, and retain only such confidential material as is necessary. It doesn't take a military genius to figure out the why behind those directives: war is coming.

In the congressional hearings after the war, the military leaders in Hawaii weren't the only ones who were charged with failures of communication. So were the military leaders in Washington. The majority report did not find Kimmel and

Short in dereliction of their duties, as they had been charged shortly after the attack, but with the lesser charge of being negligent in their duties.

These were only two of the many communications that were transmitted in the year prior to the attack. Maybe those dispatches weren't clear enough, but the recipients never replied to them, asking for clarification. Regardless, they weren't taken seriously.

Why?

The answer to that question leads to my third point.

3. We Were Overconfident

Overconfident is too generous a term. The more accurate word is *arrogant*. We just thought we knew it all. But we didn't. Among the things we didn't understand was our enemy. We knew our enemy only from afar, seeing only the color of his skin, only the shortness of his stature, and only the strangeness of his language. The sum total of those "onlies" was that we believed the Japanese were inferior. There is no better an illustration of this than when Admiral Kimmel was eating lunch with Edward Morgan, the lawyer who wrote the majority report for the congressional hearing that took place between 1945 and 1946.

> *Morgan:* Why, after you received this "war warning" message of November 27, did you leave the Fleet in Pearl Harbor?

Kimmel: All right, Morgan—I'll give you your answer. I never thought those little yellow sons-of-bitches could pull off such an attack, so far from Japan.

That conversation was off the record, and it was years later before Morgan spoke of it, but it pretty much says it all. That kind of arrogance explains why the naval base was not better prepared for the attack.

4. We Were Not Alert

The two highest officers in command at Pearl Harbor—one from the Navy, the other from the Army—didn't talk to each other about the warnings they had received. Nor did they implement their respective defensive plans, which they had rehearsed time and time again.

It is inexplicable and inexcusable.

One of the baffling aspects of their failure to prepare the base involves the alert level that was decided upon. Just as we have terror alert levels in our country since 9/11, so Pearl Harbor had graduated threat levels. Their alerts specified what the threat might be. Alert No. 1, for example, was a warning against the threat of sabotage. Protocol for that alert was clear. Strengthen patrols by submarines. Watch for suspicious people who might be spies or saboteurs. Bunch up the ships and planes to make them easier to guard if the enemy were to try to disable or destroy them.

If the base had been on higher alert—an Alert No. 3, which was a warning for the possibility of an all-out assault from the air—our planes would have been gassed up and lined up on the runway with all their munitions already loaded, ready for takeoff at a minute's notice.

If there is one overarching failure, from the top down, it was the failure to be alert. Gordon Prange wrote: "There is no substitute for alertness. The U.S. forces on Oahu were prepared in the sense of being well equipped, well trained, well led, brave, and willing to fight. But they were not on the alert, and they paid a heavy penalty."

In spite of all these failures, the attack could still have been thwarted, or at least lessened in severity, if action had been taken on three occasions that morning. Any one of them would have made a huge difference.

1. The USS *Ward* fired on an unidentified sub outside the harbor, sinking it. At 7:00 A.M. the ship reported the sinking to authorities at Pearl, but the report was passed so slowly up the chain of command that no alert was sounded. The report was made almost an hour before the attack. It was time enough to warn everyone, to get at least some of the ships out of the harbor, and to scramble our airplanes into the air, ready to engage the oncoming planes.

2. Stateside, a warning was dispatched from Washington, D.C., to Hawaii at 1 P.M. eastern time, 6:30 A.M. Hawaii time: "An almost immediate break is experienced between the United States and Japan." Although it was alleged that every effort had been made to get the message to Hawaii as soon as possible, the message arrived too late to do any good. If there had been a greater sense of urgency to send the message, there would have been enough time to muster the men and launch the aircraft.

3. The Army had recently installed a radar unit on the top of a mountain on the island, and Private Joseph Locard was monitoring it. The new device was so sensitive it could detect the whirring of an airplane engine more than one hundred miles away. Shortly after 7:00 A.M., the private, who was still in training and unaccustomed to the device, suddenly saw a huge blip on the screen. He knew they were planes, and a lot of them, and they were only 132 miles away. He jumped out of his seat and called the Army Information Center. By then there was still time to alert the island, still time to rouse the pilots and get their planes in the air, still time to alert the fleet and send men to their battle stations. But the officer on the other end of the phone told the inexperienced private that a bunch of bombers was scheduled to arrive that morning, and he said it must be them.

Here is what I would want to say to every young man or woman entering some branch of the service today: Absorb the training you receive, every bit of it; you never know what part of it you may need. An attack could happen again, anytime, anywhere. A lot of information doesn't filter down to the man at his battle station, which is why you *have* to be alert.

13

Remembering the Arizona

*Humanity cannot afford to forget the lessons of Pearl Harbor.
The world is much too small; the risk is much too great; the
time is much too late.*

—Gordon W. Prange,
Pearl Harbor: The Verdict of History

The best documentary about the *Arizona* is the Discovery
Channel's *Pearl Harbor: Death of the* Arizona. Working
with the makers of the documentary, Boeing Autometric did
a frame-by-frame analysis of film footage that Eric Haakenson had shot the moment the ship exploded. The Haakenson
film was to the destruction of the *Arizona* what the Zapruder
film was to the assassination of John F. Kennedy.

Like the forensics applied to the Zapruder film, Boeing Autometric did a detailed analysis of the Haakenson film. The discussion of the footage, along with the undersea archaeological evidence, is riveting and provides the most conclusive evidence of exactly what happened to the *Arizona*.

The Discovery Channel had committed to show the documentary in Honolulu for the sixtieth anniversary of Pearl Harbor, in 2001. The schedule was tight. It was September, and the final footage had not been shot, let alone edited. The last day of shooting took place in Washington, D.C., less than three months away from the screening in December.

On that day, September 11, 2001, director Erik Nelson met with National Park Service historian Daniel Martinez and the staff of Boeing Autometric to view the conclusions of Boeing's experts. The meeting took place in the morning. Curtains were drawn and lights were dimmed so the computer images could be better seen.

Frame by frame, they watched the *Arizona* under attack. And they did this over and over, explaining in detail what happened and when. It was clear the attack had been calculated, down to the exact engineering specs of the bomb. It had to be hard enough to penetrate the decks of the battleship. To do this, the Japanese took a bomb used by their battleships and redesigned it so it would have armor-piercing capabilities. And it had to be dropped at precisely the right altitude. If released too low, it would not have enough force to penetrate the deck, and it would be deflected into the sea. Dropped too high, and it would have too much force and would pass through all the decks and out the bottom of the hull.

As they watched the footage, they had no idea what was happening in New York City and at the Pentagon, which was only a few miles from where they were meeting. During the analysis, a Boeing staff member slipped in the back of the room, leaned over the shoulders of those huddled around the computer, and said: "We have another Pearl Harbor right now. The World Trade Center and the Pentagon have been hit, and the White House and Capitol have been evacuated."

That staff member was not the only person to immediately make the connection between 9/11 and Pearl Harbor. On the night of the attack, President George W. Bush wrote this in his diary: "The Pearl Harbor of the 21st century took place today."

Daniel Martinez, the Park Service historian who oversees the *Arizona,* and Erik Nelson, the director of the documentary, were scheduled to fly out of Washington, D.C., on the flight that had been crashed into the Pentagon. But because of the need to get the last day of filming done, they had to cancel their flight.

———

WHERE WERE YOU when 9/11 happened?

I remember where I was. I was living in Santa Maria, California, and my son called from Santa Barbara. "Turn on the TV," he said. I did, and I couldn't believe what I saw. *Why would they bomb the twin towers?* I wondered.

It was a well-coordinated attack, I later learned. Just like the attack on Pearl Harbor. The targets, just like the ones at Pearl Harbor, were specific. And their goal in demolishing the World Trade Center? To demoralize America. The same goal the Japanese had in demolishing the Pacific Fleet. But the attack on Pearl Harbor *didn't* demoralize us. It galvanized us. So did the attack on New York.

Do you remember how the country came together that day? Democrats and Republicans put aside their differences and stood in solidarity on the steps of the Capitol. Do you remember the emotions the attack evoked in you? Do you remember the buildings surrounding the emptiness where the World Trade Center towers once stood? One building in particular. I bet you can see the picture in your mind. The building had a huge expanse of white fabric that draped down from the top of the building. On it was written, WE WILL NEVER FORGET.

"REMEMBER PEARL HARBOR!" was the battle cry of sailors in the Pacific, inspiring retaliation in response to the Japanese attack on Pearl Harbor. It is also a clarion call for the United States to stay strong, stay ready, and stay alert in a world where America's enemies have the power to launch even deadlier attacks than those of that unsuspecting December morning in 1941.

The great lesson we too often learn from history, however, is that we are so prone to forget the past. And there is a price we pay for our forgetfulness.

This is why Pearl Harbor matters. It reminds us how we, too, are a target, how vulnerable we are, how it could happen all over again, at a moment when we least expect it.

Historian Gordon W. Prange spent four decades of his life researching and writing two definitive books about Pearl Harbor. The first was *At Dawn We Slept: The Untold Story of Pearl Harbor*. The second, its sequel, was *Pearl Harbor: The Verdict of History*. He was uniquely qualified for the task. During World War II he served as an officer in the Naval Reserve. After the war he continued to serve during the occupation of Japan from December 1945 to July 1951. From October 1946 to June 1951 he was chief of Douglas MacArthur's G-2 Historical Section.

Prange summed up everything he had learned from his research and writing in the last two sentences of his second book. "Humanity cannot afford to forget the lessons of Pearl Harbor. The world is much too small; the risk is much too great; the time is much too late."

———

MEMORIAL TRIBUTE
IN HONOR OF THE MEN OF THE U.S.S. ARIZONA
WHO MADE THE SUPREME SACRIFICE IN THE
DEFENSE OF OUR COUNTRY AT PEARL HARBOR
ON DECEMBER 7, 1941
WITH OUR HOPE THAT THERE SHALL BE
EVERLASTING PEACE
BETWEEN OUR COUNTRY AND JAPAN

—From a plaque that was dedicated at the
memorial by George S. Ishaida of the
United Japanese Society of Hawaii

I have visited the *Arizona* Memorial on fifteen occasions over the years. Each time, the number of my shipmates grows smaller, which makes the burden of bearing witness greater. As long as I have life, I will tell the story. A day will come, though, when I can no longer do that, when all of us survivors can no longer do that.

This is why the memorial is so important.

It keeps the story alive. The location of the memorial, the design of the structure, the etching of the names, the wording on the plaques, they all help tell the story of what happened in that harbor so many years ago. When we go there, we are reminded both of the worst of things in that story and of the best of things—of the cruelty of those who attacked our country and of the courage of those who defended it.

The design for the memorial came from the Honolulu architect Alfred Preis. The open-air structure is 184 feet long and spans the wreck about midship. The structure sags in the middle and curves upward on either end. Preis explained the meaning behind the design: "Wherein the structure sags in the center but stands strong and vigorous at the ends, expresses initial defeat and ultimate victory. . . . The overall effect is one of serenity. Overtones of sadness have been omitted to permit the individual to contemplate his own personal responses . . . his innermost feelings."

When you go to the memorial, you will find a museum and the visitor center. Both help to keep the story of Pearl Harbor alive through pictures, words, models, and objects salvaged from the ship and from the harbor. A crumpled Japanese torpedo is on display, along with a model of the plane that would have dropped it. One of the *Arizona*'s three 19,585-pound anchors is on display, along with a large clock that was salvaged from the wreck, whose hands stopped at 8:06.

Before you go to the memorial, you will watch a twenty-three-minute reenactment of the attack on a large screen. Some of the film is actual footage. The rest is from old black-and-white films that have been seamlessly spliced into the real footage. It is a gripping experience, preparing you for your encounter with the memorial.

After seeing the film, you will take a quarter-mile boat trip to the memorial. The closer the boat comes to it, the quieter the visitors become. When you step off the boat onto the dock, you step into a reverential hush that is palpable.

Out of reverence, no part of the structure touches the wreck. The only object that touches it is an American flag attached to the mast by order of Admiral Arthur W. Radford. A plaque in the area explains why:

"FROM TODAY ON THE USS *ARIZONA*
WILL AGAIN FLY OUR COUNTRY'S FLAG
AS PROUDLY AS SHE DID ON THE
MORNING OF 7 DECEMBER 1941.
I AM SURE THE *ARIZONA*'S CREW WILL
KNOW AND APPRECIATE WHAT WE ARE
DOING" ADMIRAL A. W. RADFORD, USN
7 MARCH 1950

There is something noble about what the admiral did. To understand the gesture you have to realize how much those in the military revere our flag. We have all said the Pledge of Allegiance to the flag when we were schoolkids, but who of us ever took that pledge seriously? The military takes it seriously. They not only pledge their allegiance to that flag, they *live* their allegiance. Every day they fly those colors. Every day I do, too. I proudly fly them in front of my home.

There are three parts to the memorial—the entry, the assembly room, and the shrine. The central assembly room has seven large open windows on either wall and on the ceiling, the number representing the date of the attack. The room also contains an opening in the floor where visitors can look down on the submerged deck and drop flowers there if they wish. The shrine is a simple space architecturally. A velvet rope separates the living from the dead, their names etched into the massive white marble wall. A plaque is embedded among the names. It reads:

TO THE MEMORY OF THE GALLANT MEN
HERE ENTOMBED AND THEIR SHIPMATES
WHO GAVE THEIR LIVES IN ACTION
ON DECEMBER 7, 1941

The inscription reminds us that it is a tomb we are standing above, a resting place for more than a thousand of those gallant men. It is also a place where their families can find rest, a place where they can lay down at least some of the heaviness they have been carrying all these years. I hope so. I pray so. Whenever I go to that tomb, I pray for those men. And I pray for their families.

Since 1982, the Navy has allowed survivors from the *Ar-*

izona to be interred there, along with a full military service. They can either have their ashes scattered over the wreck, or they can have their ashes put in an urn that a Navy diver will place in the barbette of the No. 2 turret.

The first time I visited the memorial was on the twenty-fifth anniversary of Pearl Harbor. I came with my wife and two sons. I didn't know what to expect. Everywhere I turned there was a reminder of what I had somehow survived. A lot of sorrow spilled out of me, and several times I had to wipe tears from my eyes. Spilling out with the sorrow were the questions. I wondered about the "why" of it all. We could have been warned about how imminent the attack was, we *should* have been warned. Why didn't the naval brass and the bigwigs in Washington not share the information they had? Why were we the last to know? And then, only afterward.

I was angry. Angry at the politicians, at the military leaders, at the officers on my own ship. Angry at the enemy. I was even angry that day with some of the visitors.

Especially *one* of them.

Mitsuo Fuchida. *Captain* Mitsuo Fuchida.

I couldn't believe he was there, at the memorial. His presence seemed a sacrilege.

Fuchida, I had learned, was the man who commanded the first wave of planes, the one who ordered his radioman to say, "To, To, To!" (short for the Japanese word *totsugekiseyo,*

meaning "charge"), which signaled the attack. He participated in the attack, but most of the time he hovered over the
area like a bird of prey catching updrafts and gliding above
the danger in lazy circles. As he did, he took photographs so
he could document the greatest defeat in U.S. naval history.

When the war ended, he retired from the military, with-
drawing even from public life to become a farmer. During
that time he grew depressed, lamenting that he had been forgotten. "I was like a star that had fallen. At one moment I
was Captain Mitsuo Fuchida, and the next, I was a nobody!"

In 1950, that changed. Fuchida became a Christian, I
learned. Through his conversion he found a way out of that
farm and into the public eye. Missionaries at the time were
evangelizing the city of Osaka, driving through the streets in
a van, speaking to them through a portable public address
system. Fuchida accompanied them and took the microphone
to announce for all to hear: "I am Mitsuo Fuchida who led
the air raid on Pearl Harbor. I have now surrendered my
heart and my life to Jesus Christ."

Following his impassioned public announcement, the local headlines read: FROM A SOLDIER OF FAME TO A SOLDIER
OF LOVE.

He came to the United States as a traveling evangelist,
speaking wherever he could, giving his testimony. He met
with Billy Graham, even fancied himself as a "small-scale

Billy Graham," to use his words. The evangelist had given Fuchida numerous opportunities to give his testimony at Graham's crusades. He toured the country, planning to make Honolulu his last stop, where he was going to place a wreath on the *Arizona*. It was a calculated move, strategically planned. By this time he had a documentary film in the works, and his photo had been on the front page of the *New York Times*. People were reading about him. Soon they would be seeing a film about him. His star was rising, and he was ecstatic.

On December 6, 1966, the night before the ceremony at the memorial, Fuchida was at a dinner party in the home of the editor of the local Honolulu newspaper. The evening, understandably, was awkward. Kendall J. Fielder, who had been chief of Army Intelligence in 1941, was among the awkward ones. He tried his best, but he just couldn't muster the words that Fuchida undoubtedly had hoped to hear. Fielder tried to find the right ones, but all he could say was: "You try to forgive and forget." He paused short of forgiveness, as if it were a bridge too far. All he could say was, "I lost a lot of friends that day."

We *all* lost a lot of friends that day. And we never recovered from it. Yes, our wounds healed, most of them anyway. And we learned to walk again. But we walked with a limp. And we walked with a limp for the rest of our lives. Most of our limps you couldn't see. You never would have known by looking at us that we had them.

The next morning, Fuchida arrived early at the *Arizona* Memorial, bringing a film crew with him, along with a few of his fellow pilots who had survived the war. He met with some of our survivors, including twelve who had been on the *Arizona*. Members of his entourage wanted the survivors to stand with him for a group photograph and shake hands as a gesture of reconciliation.

I could not believe what was happening. To me, it was a desecration of a holy shrine, turning the sacredness of the memorial into something as profane as a photo op. Many of our men refused to be a part of the profanity. A journalist asked if I was going to pose with Fuchida. I shook my head no. The man asked why. And I couldn't hold my anger in any longer.

"There's no way I'm gonna shake their hands. And I know a thousand other men who wouldn't either." I could have said more. Were I not a Christian myself, I *would* have said more. But I didn't.

The Japanese company that manufactured the Zero was Mitsubishi. Today they make cars, many of which are sold in the United States. On some level, if only an economic level, we have made peace with our enemy, and they with us.

Why can't I?

Jesus said to love your enemies, to pray for those who persecute you, to forgive anyone who has wronged you, so that your Father who is in Heaven may also forgive you your trespasses.

A part of me wishes I could.

Another part wants to take the stand to testify on behalf of those whose voices were silenced by that unconscionable trespass against us. If you had only been there—if you had seen so many of your shipmates reduced to unidentifiable body parts, young men barely out of high school, even younger—you would understand.

Let me tell you something I read about another anniversary. It may help you to see it from a different perspective, from the perspective of the servicemen who were attacked that day and saw so many of their shipmates slaughtered. It was the fifty-ninth anniversary of Pearl Harbor, and a group that called themselves "The World War II American and Japanese Friendship Committee" had arranged for a "reconciliation" ceremony on the deck of the USS *Missouri,* the ship where the Japanese signed the documents for an unconditional surrender. About one hundred Japanese veterans were to be there, along with three Japanese pilots who had participated in the slaughter. American veterans and survivors of Pearl Harbor were invited to attend. The hope of the organizers was that the two groups would come together and shake hands. Sterling Cale, a survivor of Pearl Harbor, planned to attend. His wife, though, who came from a Filipino-American family on the island, refused to go with him, giving him this ultimatum instead. "I don't want to see any photographs of you shaking hands with them."

Another survivor, Ray Emory, reacted even more strongly:

"Look, if my next-door neighbor raped and murdered my mother fifty years ago, do you think that I'd be inviting him over for lunch?" Ray had been in charge of identifying the bodies of the dead who were listed as "unknowns." A gruesome job. Unimaginable how difficult it must have been.

Ray's reaction captures how so many survivors felt about reconciling with their enemy. That is certainly how *I* felt. The men they butchered, these young men who were barely out of high school, let me tell you about them. They wrote to their mothers. They sent money home to help out their families. And so many of them went ashore that weekend, looking for a Christmas present to send to their kid brother or sister. They were young men with a sparkle in their eyes and a future just waiting for them to step into and do something wonderful with their lives.

The boys in the band, for example.

Before I left the memorial that December day in 1966, I stood at the railing, staring at the water, watching a black tear making its way to the surface, where it dispersed into a rainbow of colors that caught the sun. I said a prayer for the gallant men entombed there. And a prayer for their families.

But not for Fuchida.

Fifty years have passed. So has Fuchida. When I go to the seventy-fifth anniversary, will the Lord grant me the grace to do what I could not do for the past three-quarters of a century?

14

Preparing for the Seventy-Fifth Anniversary

Telling their story is telling our story as well. If we don't keep telling the story, keep reminding people that these guys were there, that they sacrificed everything, they're going to fade away. . . . These guys gave up almost everything in their lives for our country to be as free as it is.

—Nikki Stratton, my granddaughter

The commemoration of the seventy-fifth anniversary of Pearl Harbor is guided by the theme "Honoring Our Past, Inspiring Our Future." The words are drawn from a keynote address given by General Lori Robinson, commander of the Pacific Air Forces on the seventy-third anniversary.

Coming back to Pearl Harbor always has been an important way for me to honor our past. One time when I came back, I tried to find if there were any remains of my battle station. The superstructure of the ship, which had been cut away, lies in the boneyard of Ford Island, I discovered. I went to see it—or what was left of it. It's back in the jungle, camouflaged by overgrowth. When I got there, I found it had been cordoned off, as if it were a crime scene.

It seemed so weak, lying there, rusting away. If someone were to stumble upon it, who would even know what it was that lies there so crippled? Who would know its name, its function, or the story behind it, how it ended up where it is?

It once served on the greatest ship in the greatest navy of the greatest nation on earth.

That is its story.

It's a shame it has been relegated to a junk heap in the Navy's backyard. It carries so much history, yet it is cared for so little.

December 2016 will likely be my last time to go back. I look forward to reuniting with several Pearl Harbor survivors at the anniversary, especially the other four survivors from the *Arizona:*

Lauren Bruner, ninety-six, from La Mirada, California
Lou Conter, ninety-five, from Grass Valley, California

Lonnie Cook, ninety-five, from Morris, California

Ken Potts, ninety-four, from Provo, Utah

Our ranks are thinning. With each passing anniversary, there are fewer of us. We lost three in the last year.

Seaman First Class Clarendon "Clare" Hetrick was the youngest living survivor when he died in April 2016 in Las Vegas, a month shy of his ninety-third birthday. He was the sixth of twelve children born to Elmer and Hazel Hetrick in Cheyenne, Wyoming. He started as a mess cook, then moved to shuttling munitions to the ship's big guns. When the *Arizona* started sinking, he made his way to the edge of the ship, looking for a rescue vessel to come his way. None did. Although he couldn't swim, he swam *that* day, jumping into the water and dog-paddling to Ford Island. He stayed in the Pacific Theater, and was wounded at Iwo Jima. In 1949 he left the Navy and finished his military service in the Air Force, retiring in 1961. He was at the reunion in 2015 that was held in Tucson at the University of Arizona. He came in a wheelchair. But he came. Full of vigor and determination, he toasted his fallen shipmates. And when the time came for the ceremonial tolling of the bell in their honor, he gripped the rope, along with Lauren Bruner, and rang it. "I am ready to go back again," he told a reporter. "I'll go back any way I can." He will go back this year to Honolulu, but it will not be in a wheelchair; it will be in an urn. His ashes will be interred on the *Arizona* with his fellow shipmates.

Coxswain Raymond John Haerry died September 27, 2015, at his home in Rhode Island. He was ninety-four. He never returned to Pearl Harbor. The memories were just too horrific for him. His son, Raymond Haerry Jr., said his father never wanted to talk about the nightmare he lived through that day, but he was able to piece together this much of his father's story: he was running to get ammunition for his anti-aircraft gun when the blast from the armor-piercing bomb blew him overboard, where he swam through the flaming water, pushing his arms in front of him to sweep away the flames until he reached Ford Island.

Boatswain's Mate Second Class John Anderson was the oldest survivor when he died in 2015 at the age of ninety-eight. Complications from hip surgery, I was told. His ashes will be buried with his shipmates in a ceremony at the memorial, along with Hetrick's. This will be the first time that two survivors are interred at the same time. Anderson stayed aboard as our ship began to sink, helping others get off, all the while looking for his twin brother. A senior officer, who must have been Fuqua, shoved him into a boat that was taking men to Ford Island. John obeyed the order, but once he was let off, he stepped into another boat and went back to the ship. He just couldn't give up looking.

He never did find his brother. It was the biggest heartache of his life.

There were thirty-seven sets of brothers on board, if you can believe it. Only one full set of brothers survived the attack: Ken and Russell Warriner. Ken was away at flight school, and Russell, though badly burned, pulled through.

And there was one father-and-son pair: Thomas Free and his son William Free. Both died.

Can you imagine losing your husband *and* your son on the same day?

How parents must have felt when they got the telegram— like the one Clyde Nelson's folks received—breaking the news that both of their sons were dead. Or all *three* of their sons? Some parents had a trio of children on the *Arizona*.

In spite of the heartache I live with, I loved being a sailor, and I would go back and enlist all over again if I could. On December 7, 2016, I will be going back to where I served, so many years ago. My family is coming with me. My wife, Velma. My son Randy, along with his daughters, Nikki and Jessika. And the children from my deceased son, Robert— Robert Jr., Dana, and Kimberly. Five grandkids in all.

I am excited about the possibility of us five *Arizona* survivors getting to go in a miniature, two-man sub and explore the ship's hull. A handful of divers have explored her, mostly from the outside, but they have gone into the ship as far as the officers' quarters, salvaging a few things they found there. I am told that you can see into the captain's quarters and find his dress uniform still on its hanger, ready to wear, complete with its medals.

This year I am most excited, though, about meeting Joe George's daughter, who will be there. Several of us lobbied to get the Medal of Honor for her father for the heroics he demonstrated that morning in saving the six of us. So far we have been unsuccessful. The biggest reason is that the Navy doesn't want to honor someone who disobeyed his superior officer. But had he been a more compliant person, more respectful of authority, I wouldn't have lived to tell the story. None of us who climbed across that line to the *Vestal* would have.

Two of those who Joe saved, Lauren Bruner and I, are the only ones still living. Now, even Joe George is dead. I never met him. I can't wait to express my appreciation to his daughter for her dad saving my life. And I can't wait to show her the generations who have lived because of that one act of valor. Of all the gallant men on our ship, he stands tallest. At least to me. And I know five other men who would feel the same way. In an interview later in his life, Joe said, "We got those men on board, but I don't think they made it."

I wish I could tell him, "We *did* make it, Joe, thanks to you." I am sure I would hug him. And though I am not a crier, I am sure I would tear up as I introduced him, one by one, to my family.

WHEN I GO back to the memorial, I visit to pay my respects. I have no animosity for the Japanese people. The Japanese military, well, that's another thing. I still have so much anger toward them.

I recently read the words of Rabbi Tzvi Freeman to a woman who had lost her son. She struggled with grief and anger, she told him. She had "somewhat made peace," she told him. Somewhat, but not completely. She told the rabbi she had read a quotation that she sensed had meaning for her, but she couldn't figure out what exactly it was.

The quotation was from a Jewish holy man named Baal Shem Tov: "In remembrance is the secret of redemption."

Then she asked: "Could you help me to understand the connection between remembrance and redemption?"

The rabbi responded tenderly to the woman, expressing his sincere condolences for the loss of her son. "Each moment in life," he told her, "taken on its own, is imprisoned. It is a fragment, and as such, orphaned from any meaning, like torn pages of a book scattered by the wind. Remembrance creates a . . . wholeness in which all things are redeemed and complete."

He went on to mention how the Exodus from Egypt was

something that the Jewish people were told to remember. Passover is their way of doing that. It is how they remember the past and how they pass that memory on to their children.

"In terms of your situation," he told her, "the point at which your child was lost, I'm sure, was impossibly painful. Experiences such as these become barriers between the present and the past."

He went on to share with her a story from his days as a student.

I remember a music professor who would start the class by playing a chord on the piano and asking us to write down the notes. The chords became more and more sophisticated as the class progressed: minor 9ths, suspended, augmented, 13ths. . . . Then, one day, he played the ugliest chord imaginable—and this time, not only were we asked to write the notes, but to tell him the era and composer, as well.

All were convinced it was post-Wagnerian. Most placed it as "modern ugly—likely from the 1920s." Several suggested Arnold Schönberg.

Then he played us the entire piece. It was a fugue from J. S. Bach's Well-Tempered Clavichord. The voices of the fugue fought their way into a crescendo of complexity culminating in the agonizing tension of that chord . . . and then smoothly resolved back into the sweetest baroque harmony.

Of course, it was all beautiful. But the most beautiful was that which we had first heard as the most ugly.

The rabbi told the bereaved mother, "May we all merit to hear the entire symphony fulfilled, sooner than we can imagine."

The rabbi concluded his words to the woman: "May we all be reunited again very soon in the world to come."

I have a hard time finding any redemption in my remembrances of what happened to us on that horrible December day. Maybe someday, in the world to come, the larger symphony will be made clear.

The way I see it, though, we remember Pearl Harbor for the same reason the Jewish people remember the Holocaust, or the American people remember 9/11—so it will never happen again. Not on *my* watch. And, I pray, not on yours, either.

We also remember it in order to hallow the memories of those who were lost. And that, I believe, is how past and present are connected, through remembrance.

That is how I would like to conclude my words to you. May we all be reunited again very soon in the world to come. All the gallant men of the *Arizona*. And all the other gallant men who died on that date that lives in infamy.

And Fuchida?

Thomas Wolfe, in *You Can't Go Home Again,* wrote that

to die is "to lose the earth you know for greater knowing; to lose the life you have, for greater life; to leave the friends you have loved, for greater loving; to find a land more kind than home, more large than earth." I am a person of faith. As I said, I have been told that after the war ended, Mitsuo Fuchida converted to Christianity. If that is true, we will meet again someday in the land that is more kind than home, more large than earth. I will leave the life I have lived for the past ninety-four years, for greater life. Leave the friends I have loved, for greater loving. There I will meet the enemies I could not forgive in this life. And there I will find a heart that is larger, more forgiving.

Then we shall shake hands, Mitsuo and me.

Until then, with the rabbi I pray: "May we all be reunited again very soon in the world to come."

And with my mama I pray: "May the good Lord have mercy on us all."

Epilogue

The Reunion

"Have I lived a good life?"

—Private James Francis Ryan,
in *Saving Private Ryan*

The film *Saving Private Ryan* is perhaps the greatest war movie ever made, in my opinion. Why? Because it tells the truth about war. Not many movies, especially older movies, have told the truth about what war is *really* like, about how terrifying it is when you are in the chaotic middle of it, getting shot at, your fellow soldiers or shipmates dropping all around you, and you know there is nothing you can do to help them because you have to take out the enemy if the slaughter is ever to stop.

The film is bookended by two scenes of an older James

Francis Ryan at the Allied cemetery at Normandy. The first occurs at the beginning of the film, when Ryan wanders through a field of white crosses, searching for someone. His wife and adult children follow him. We don't know who he is searching for, but we can tell by the expression on his face that finding that person's grave is of the utmost importance.

We see a close-up of Ryan's eyes, and the filmmaker transitions us to the invasion of Normandy, where a Higgins boat is about to land on Omaha Beach. And for the next twenty-three minutes, we are given a sense of what it was like to be on that beach so many years ago. The rest of the movie shows us who Ryan was searching for in that cemetery. He was looking for the grave of Captain Miller, the man who gave his life trying to find Ryan and take him home.

At the end of the story, the filmmaker brings us back to the present, to that same cemetery, to the grave that Ryan has now found. He stands before it, not knowing what to say, what to do. His family watches, a respectful distance away.

Having been through the story with him, we know why finding that grave was so important. Standing before the grave of his captain, his eyes brim with emotion. Finally he gathers himself, stands erect, and salutes.

His wife comes to his side, unsure what to say, how to help. Ryan turns to her and asks, "Have I lived a good life?"

An odd question, it seems. But at this point in that old soldier's life, it is the only question that matters.

Maybe you have to go to war to understand that moment in the movie. Or maybe you just have to be at a place where you have more of your life behind you than you have in front of you. I have been to war, and am now well into my tenth decade of life, and I can tell you, it *is* the only question that matters.

You wonder if you will be remembered when you are gone, wonder who will remember you and why. And you realize that what *really* matters is the family that goes with you to that place halfway around the world where a part of you was buried so many years ago.

It is what mattered to James Ryan when he went to that cemetery to remember a painful part of his past. It is what matters to me when I go to that sunken cemetery to remember a painful part of my own past.

Have I lived a good life?

NOT LONG AGO, after completing the paperwork for a firearms permit at the El Paso County Sheriff's Office, I approached the counter for fingerprinting. But they had trouble reading my prints. Because of my burns, the skin on my fingers is almost all smooth, lacking most of the swirls necessary to identify me. It was almost comical how many times they tried to get a readable print. They finally got enough of a swirl on the edge of one finger, and I got the permit.

I look at my son Randy, hoping that I have left some discernible prints on his life. Something he can look at and say, "I got that from my dad." I hope I have imprinted some swirl of who I am on the lives of my grandchildren too.

And Velma. What can I say about my bride of sixty-seven years? *Her* fingerprints are all over me, I can tell you that. She has loved me so long, and so well.

Can I tell you how we met?

At a carnival. It was a small carnival that had come to Red Cloud. It had a merry-go-round, Ferris wheel, lots of booths where you could throw a ball to knock down bowling pins, toss coins for a chance to win a stuffed animal, those kinds of things. It was light outside when I met her. I still remember the late-afternoon sun on her hair. Gosh, she was pretty. She was there with a girlfriend. I was there with my cousin Jack, and suddenly wishing I had come alone. I had seen her around town occasionally, and at the bank where she worked.

I finally got the courage to ask her to a dance in Rivertown, and we started dating after that. She told me she was from a little town called Bladen, twenty miles away. Her parents were farmers there. She graduated in 1943 and moved to Hastings, Nebraska, to become a nurse, but she decided nursing wasn't for her, and so she moved to Red Cloud in 1945. She worked in Blue Hill as a Linotype operator for a while. She had printer's ink on her hands all the time, and she would cover them up by wearing gloves whenever she went out.

I covered up in my own way. I mostly wore slacks and long-sleeved shirts so she had no occasion to ask me about my scars. She knew I had served in the Navy, but I didn't talk about the war. Didn't want to think about it. So we spoke about other things, and before long we had small-talked our way into each other's heart.

For me, it was love at first sight.

I remember one day blurting out, "You would be awful easy to fall in love with."

She blurted out nothing. But she did smile, and she thanked me.

Mostly we went to the movies. Red Cloud had a nice theater, the one at which I used to work. And when a band would come through town, we'd go to the dance where they were playing.

She was a good dancer. I was not.

There was a lot she was that I wasn't.

She was romantic. I was not.

And yet, six months later we were engaged. I got her a ring, but it was a small, cheap one, which was all I could afford. We were married in the home of her cousin, who was a woman and also the minister who performed the ceremony. We took my dad's car on our honeymoon and mostly visited relatives on my side of the family. That was 1950.

She never saw my back until the honeymoon. Even then, she didn't ask about it. Not much, anyway. The scars still itched a lot, and she used to take a hairbrush and scratch my back with it. I was pretty self-conscious about them, even after we were married, and that's why I wore long-sleeved shirts all the time. I don't think I ever wore a short-sleeved shirt until we moved to California.

I left the Navy when the war ended. But I never quit the sea. All the time I was in Red Cloud, I couldn't wait to get back to it. I think Velma was ready for a change, too.

We headed west, to California. I had a buddy in Bakersfield named Clarence Dobson. Remember me telling you about Dobby, the one I went through Mare Island with? Velma and I stayed with him and his wife until I found a job in Santa Barbara. It was hard to leave, but I was ready to go.

We moved to Santa Barbara, and we lived there for thirty years. Along the way, we had four kids.

Robert, he was the oldest. Born February 10, 1951; died July 28, 2007. He had served in Vietnam, and he passed of complications from hepatitis C and Agent Orange exposure.

Randy was our second child. Born July 12, 1954; died 2013, of a heart attack. Fortunately, he didn't stay dead. He had called 911, but by the time the paramedics reached him, his heart had stopped. Thank the good Lord, they brought him back.

Gypsy Dawn came into the world not completely developed. She lived for three days.

Roxanne Jo was our other girl. She lived for five.

Randy lives near us in Colorado Springs, where he has worked for the postal service for thirty-seven years. His true vocation, though, has been helping high school girls get basketball scholarships. He played college ball himself, and basketball is to him what the sea was to me. He loves it. Both his daughters played college ball, and Jessica coaches at Valor Christian High School in Denver. He has helped around 170 young women get full scholarships, many of them to Division I schools.

While we lived in Santa Barbara, I served as an able seaman offshore and as a deep-sea diver for Treen's Commercial Diving. While working for them, I laid down big server lines on the bottom of the ocean, from five to seven miles offshore. I probably laid 1,100 joints of pipe that were six to eight feet long, with an inside diameter of 11 feet. I once dived in a miniature sub 1,100 feet deep. Few people at the time had been to 1,000.

I later took a job setting up oil drilling platforms in Anchorage, Alaska. I worked with the divers, running the phone lines, talking with them, monitoring how they were doing. When they surfaced, I monitored them in the decompression chambers.

I saved a diver once. He had stayed down too long, and

his oxygen was running out. On top of that, he got tangled in some debris on the bottom. I was told not to give him more oxygen, because he would get the bends on the way up, and that would kill him. The way I looked at it, I would rather have to deal with the nitrogen narcosis on the surface than deal with a diver who couldn't breathe on the bottom of the ocean. I gave him more air, then dropped a basket down for him to get into so we could carry him up. We had to put him straight into the decompression chamber, and he did go through a lot of pain, but he lived.

I was on a diving job when I heard the news about President Kennedy being assassinated. It hit me really hard. I liked the president, a lot. It helped that he was a Pacific war vet like me, and had seen action in some of the same waters I had with the *Stack*. I thought he was doing a helluva job. He knew what the country needed. When he said, "Ask not what your country can do for you, ask what you can do for your country," it was just what we needed to hear. I felt we were on the right track as a nation with him behind the wheel.

I helped erect half a dozen or so drilling platforms. We drove pilings for the structures, fifty feet deep, sometimes deeper, working off a floating barge that could lift seven hundred tons.

I later worked on pipeline hookups in Chile, South America, and offshore of Colombia and Nicaragua.

I worked on several blowouts offshore of Santa Barbara,

sending divers down to cap oil leaks. It was pretty intense work, especially for the divers, because thousands of gallons of oil were leaking out, and it was their job to cap the leak. Eventually, work with divers slowed, then petered out altogether.

When that happened, we moved to Yuma, Arizona, to be near our son. I retired then, played a lot of golf, planted gardens, looked after fifteen fruit trees, mostly apple and tangelo. We lived there fifteen years, but we wearied of it and moved to Santa Maria. Our son Robert was living in our house in Santa Barbara, and when he died, we moved to Colorado Springs to be around our other son, Randy, and his family. We have lived here eight years, and I think it's safe to say that Colorado Springs was our last move.

Although I have the option to have my ashes buried on the Arizona, along with thirty-eight others whose ashes have been buried there, I won't be doing that. I will be interred where our two daughters are buried, in Nebraska . . . looking forward to the day when we can be reunited again in the world to come. . . .

. . . Robert, too.

TO THE ETERNAL MEMORY
OF OUR GALLANT SHIPMATES
IN THE USS *ARIZONA*
WHO GAVE THEIR LIVES IN ACTION
7 DECEMBER 1941

MAY GOD MAKE HIS FACE
TO SHINE UPON THEM
AND GRANT THEM PEACE

Writer's Postscript

Don's story came to me as a gift.

I had relocated to Los Angeles to try to sell several projects I had written. But nothing sold, and I was feeling a little disheartened when . . .

I got a phone call from my oldest daughter, Gretchen, who lives in the Colorado Springs, Colorado, area. She was so excited she couldn't get the words out quick enough. "Dad, I just heard a man interviewed on the radio who was a survivor from the USS *Arizona*—you know the one that was sunk at Pearl Harbor—and his name's Don Stratton and Dad his story's great and the interviewer said he was amazed it hadn't been made into a movie and Dad he lives here in Colorado Springs and he hasn't written a book, either, and he lives in Colorado Springs and Dad you'd be the perfect one to do it so what do you think?"

I was so touched by her call that I checked the story out on the Internet. Sure enough, there was a Don Stratton who was a survivor from the USS *Arizona,* and sure enough, he did live in Colorado Springs. His address and phone number were there, too, so I called him, saying something like, "Is this Don Stratton? . . . I'm Ken Gire. I'm a writer, and you don't know me, but . . ."

And I told him the story I just told you, about my daughter calling me, and I asked if he had any interest in writing a book about his experience. He said he had wanted to for some time, but he didn't have a writer to do it. My literary agent, Greg Johnson, lives in a suburb of Denver, and I asked Don if my agent and I could stop by and visit with him about the possibility of working together.

Greg and I met with Don, his wife, and his son, and when we got to hear more of his story, we were both genuinely and deeply moved. Which is what every writer wants to feel about a story he writes. What every agent wants to feel, too.

As it turned out, the seventy-fifth anniversary of Pearl Harbor, December 7, 2016, was approaching, and I talked to my agent about getting the book out before the anniversary. He said publishers don't like to rush a book because it's a lot of pressure on everyone, and they have enough pressure as it is. But, he said, you never know. . . .

Long story short, Peter Hubbard at HarperCollins loved it, wanted it, bought it.

I met with Don several times. He and his wife, Velma, were so gracious to me. His son Randy, too. One of the days when I came to Don's house to interview him, it was Velma's ninetieth birthday. A vase with eighteen red, long-stem roses sat on the counter.

And he says he's not romantic.

When I was finished interviewing him, I asked Don how he would like to be remembered. He said, "That I had led a good life, as a Christian. That I had a wonderful family. And that I was one of the people who defended our country in time of crisis." He paused a beat, then added, "One of the many."

That pause told me so much about him. He is not a person who likes attention. And he's not a person to take credit for what he's done. If there is credit due him, it's always a shared credit. He never takes it for himself.

Don Stratton is one of the last of the greatest generation. Being around him and his wife was a gift, too. Not just the story. Them. It felt so good to be able to use my skills as a writer to serve such a man and to tell such a story. In the process, I was touched by both, the story and the man. I am so grateful.

When I asked what message he would like to leave behind, he said: "That people would remember Pearl Harbor so that it would never happen again."

I truly hope Don's story does that.

It did that for me.

I hope it did that for you, too.

Thank you for taking the time to read the book.

And Gretchen, thank you, sweetheart. I love you ten bags full!

Ken Gire

P. P. S. Besides my daughter and Don, there are two others I would like to acknowledge.

Peter Hubbard, executive editor at William Morrow/HarperCollins.

He loved the story from the moment he read the proposal, making a pre-emptive offer to secure it for his publishing house. He worked tirelessly for the book you now hold in your hands, fighting for everything from the title to the cover design, and for every word in three sets of revisions. I have never worked with a finer editor.

Greg Johnson, founder of WordServe Literary.

He is the best agent I know. And he is a better person than he is an agent. He has been one of the great friends of my life. Because of him, I am a better man; and without him, the book you now hold in your hands would have never been written.

Acknowledgments

Ken Gire and his daughter, Gretchen Anthony.

Greg Johnson, our literary agent at WordServe Literary.

Peter Hubbard, our editor and champion at William Morrow.

My son Randy.

Special thanks to Joe George and Clarence "Dobby" Dobson.

To all the doctors, nurses, and medics who treated so many of us.

And to the special ladies who gave blood.

Corroborating Sources

Frontispiece quote is from *The Complete Works of Samuel Taylor Coleridge*, ed. by Professor W. G. T. Shedd (New York: Harper & Brothers, 1884), p. 380.

Prologue: The Awakening

The origin of the Yamamoto quote at the beginning of the chapter is obscure. The quote was first used in the film *Tora! Tora! Tora!* It appears that Darryl Zanuck and Elmo Williams from Twentieth Century-Fox insisted on a wrap-up scene with Yamamoto making a speech. The screenwriter, Larry Forrester, came up with the quote. Williams spoke with Forrester about the source of the quote, and Forrester said it was from a letter written by Yamamoto. Forrester died in Northridge, California, in 1968, and the source apparently died with him. There is no verifiable written source for the quote. Akira Iriye, professor of history at Harvard University, said, "Whether Yamamoto ever uttered the words, we never know. . . . In any event, what he does say in the movie becomes truth." This research is from Hiroshi Tasogawa, *All the Emperor's Men: Kuro-sawa's Pearl Harbor* (Atlanta: Applause, 2012).

The account of Roosevelt dictating his speech to his secretary is noted by Nathan Miller, *FDR: An Intimate History* (New York: Double-day, 1983), p. 477.

The original draft of the "Date of Infamy Speech" resides in the Grace Tully Archive, Franklin Delano Roosevelt Presidential Library and Museum, Hyde Park, New York. Franklin D. Roosevelt, "To the Congress of the United States," The White House, December 8, 1941.

You can see black-and-white footage of FDR's speech in its entirety on YouTube: "Periscope Film LLC: FDR Declares War (12/8/41)."

The background and atmosphere of President Roosevelt's speech are chronicled in Craig Shirley, "The Eighth of December," in *December 1941: 31 Days that Changed America and Saved the World* (Nashville, TN: Thomas Nelson, 2011), pp. 154–82.

The one dissenting vote in the House was cast by pacifist Jeannette Rankin, from Montana, who had also voted no on the Declara-tion of War in 1917. Following the vote, she told reporters, "As a woman I can't go to war and I refuse to send anyone else." Rankin was ridiculed for her vote and eventually pressured out of office by her peers. Shirley, *December 1941*, pp. 169, 170.

I have listed a handful of names of the men who served with me on the USS *Arizona*. For a complete list, see T. J. Cooper, *The USS Arizona Men: 75th Anniversary* (published by the author, Febru-ary 6, 2016).

The story of my shipmate John Evans was from an interview with him conducted February 25, 1998, by John Chalkley, Grapevine, Texas, University of North Texas, Oral History Collection, No. 1220, p. 6.

1: A Child of the Depression

The quote at the beginning of the chapter is from John Steinbeck, *The Grapes of Wrath* (New York: Viking Books, 1939), p. 3.

The quote about the woman from my hometown of Invale was from Timothy Egan, *The Worst Hard Time* (New York: Houghton Miflin Company, 2006), pp. 2-3.

The diary entries are from Timothy Egan, *The Worst Hard Time* (New York: Houghton Miflin Company, 2006), pp. 296-297.

The writings about how the depression affected farmers in Webster County, Nebraska, where I am from, are from Donald Hartwell's unpublished diary, which is on file at the Nebraska State Historical Society, Lincoln, Nebraska.

2: To Sea on the *Arizona*

The quote at the beginning of the chapter is from Molly Kent, *USS Arizona's Last Band* (Kansas City, KS: Silent Song, 1996), p. 5.

The story about Joe George's fight and subsequent court-martial is from an interview with Joe George, August 5, 1978, by Ronald E. Marcello in Little Rock, Arkansas, North Texas State University, Oral History Collection, No. 448, pp. 21–26.

The story of George throwing us a line from the *Vestal* is corroborated in an interview with Joe George, August 5, 1978, by Ronald E. Marcello in Little Rock, Arkansas, North Texas State University, Oral History Collection, No. 448, pp. 30–31.

Confirmation about the process of holystoning is in Joy Waldron Jasper, James P. Delgado, and Jim Adams, *The USS Arizona: The Ship, the Men, the Pearl Harbor Attack, and the Symbol That Aroused America* (New York: St. Martin's Press, 2001), p. 36.

Descriptions of Oahu during 1941 were confirmed by Thurston
  Clarke, *Pearl Harbor Ghosts: The Legacy of December 7, 1941*
  (New York: Ballantine, 1991), pp. 33–36.

Descriptions of Hotel Street is corroborated by Henry Berry, *This Is
  No Drill: Living Memories of the Attack on Pearl Harbor* (New
  York: Berkeley Books, 1992), pp. 110–11. Also Clarke, *Pearl Har-
  bor Ghosts,* pp. 83–92.

For a photograph of the "river of white," and for the only known
  photograph of some of the ladies of Hotel Street, posing in front
  of the Senator Hotel, see the book by Rhys Thomas, *Hotel Street
  Harry* (Highland Park, Illinois: RCT Publishing, 2016), pp. 8, 10.

For a first-hand account of a sailor on leave at Hotel Street, see the
  book by Edward C. Raymer, *Descent into Darkness*: Pearl Harbor, 1941: A Navy Diver's Memoir (Annapolis, Maryland: Naval
  Institute Press, 1996), pp. 60-71.

Details about the collision between the *Oklahoma* and the *Arizona*
  were confirmed by Kent, *USS* Arizona's *Last Band,* p. 183.

Eyewitness accounts of the collision between the *Oklahoma* and the
  Arizona are from Jasper, Delgado, and Adams, *The USS* Arizona,
  pp. 78–81.

The Lahaina incident can be found in Jasper, Delgado, and Adams,
  The USS Arizona, pp. 82–83.

Information about the repairs that the *Vestal* was scheduled to per-
  form on the *Arizona* is confirmed by Kent, *USS* Arizona's *Last
  Band,* p. 202.

3: The Last Night
The quote at the beginning of the chapter is from the film *Casablanca,*
  1942, Warner Bros., directed by Michael Curtiz.

Details of the various shops on the *Vestal* were confirmed by one of
the sailors on the ship, Frank Dolan, from an interview with him
on December 15, 1995, by Ronald E. Marcello in Jacksonville,
Texas, North Texas State University, Oral History Collection,
No. 1111, pp. 4–5.

The quote by Clarke Beach is from Thurston Clarke, *Pearl Harbor
Ghosts: The Legacy of December 7, 1941* (New York: Ballantine,
1991), p. 67.

The quote by Frank Knox is from Clarke, *Pearl Harbor Ghosts,* p. 65.

The complacent mood of the military is noted by Clarke, *Pearl Harbor
Ghosts,* p. 68.

4: December 7th

The quote at the beginning of the chapter is from Gordon W. Prange,
At Dawn We Slept: The Untold Story of Pearl Harbor (New York:
Penguin Books, 1981), p. 499.

The times are, for the most part, approximations. Everything happened so fast. We were hit so hard from so many directions, and
we were all scrambling to fight back that I had no sense of time.
It seemed like an eternity, though. I did find a minute-by-minute
breakdown of the day that was consistent with my own recollections, only more precise. I varied from it in only a few instances.
It can be found in Michael Slackman's book, *Target Pearl Harbor* (Honolulu: University of Hawaii Press and Arizona Memorial
Museum Association, 1990), pp. 285–95. He notes on page 289,
parenthetically—"(all times approximate)."

Slackman received degrees in history from the University of California at Berkeley and San Diego State University. He also worked as
a consulting historian for the U.S. Navy and the National Parks

Service. He has published extensively on Pearl Harbor, including the books, *Remembering Pearl Harbor* and *Pearl Harbor in Perspective.*

I also relied on Gordon W. Prange's research from his book, *At Dawn We Slept:* The Untold Story of Pearl Harbor (NY: Penguin Books, 1981). At times when the two sources weren't odds, I deferred to Prange, who is regarded as the most scholarly authority on Pearl Harbor.

The details for 3:57 A.M. were from Gordon W. Prange, *At Dawn We Slept:* The Untold Story of Pearl Harbor (New York: Penguin Books, 1981), pp. 495–97.

The details for 5:50 A.M. were from Gordon W. Prange, *At Dawn We Slept:* The Untold Story of Pearl Harbor (New York: Penguin Books, 1981), p. 490.

The details for 6:10–6:20 A.M. were from Gordon W. Prange, *At Dawn We Slept:* The Untold Story of Pearl Harbor (New York: Penguin Books, 1981), p. 491.

"Of 185 planes scheduled for the first wave, 183 had taken off—43 fighters, 49 high-level bombers, 51 dive bombers, and 40 torpedo planes. It was the fastest launch on record, marred by the loss of 2 fighters. One crashed on takeoff, but a destroyer quickly rescued the pilot. The second, from *Kaga*, developed engine trouble and had to be left behind."

The details for 6:30 A.M. The breakdown of specific ships can be found in Appendix B of Michael Slackman's book, *Target Pearl Harbor* (Honolulu: University of Hawaii Press and Arizona Memorial Museum Association, 1990), pp. 304–5. See also p. 22.

The details for 6:45 A.M. are from Gordon W. Prange, *At Dawn We Slept:* The Untold Story of Pearl Harbor (NY: Penguin Books, 1981), pp. 495–98.

The details for 7:00 A.M. Opana Radar Station and 7:10 A.M. are from Michael Slackman's book, *Target Pearl Harbor* (Honolulu: University of Hawaii Press and Arizona Memorial Museum Association, 1990), pp. 73–74.

The details for 7:00 A.M. second wave. The source for the planes in the second wave: Michael Slackman's book, *Target Pearl Harbor* (Honolulu: University of Hawaii Press and Arizona Memorial Museum Association, 1990), p. 72.

The quotes about the sighting of a periscope outside of Pearl Harbor is from Prange, *At Dawn We Slept*, p. 484.

The details about the duties of the band members at their battle stations was provided by Molly Kent, *USS Arizona's Last Band* (Kansas City, KS: Silent Song, 1996), pp. 221–22.

The description of twisted parts of metal and parts of bodies raining down after the explosion that sank the ship is confirmed by an interview with Martin Matthews, August 2, 1978, by Ronald E. Marcello in Richardson, Texas, North Texas State University, Oral History Collection, No. 430, pp. 28, 32.

The description of the chaos going on below the port antiaircraft director was from an interview with Clay H. Musick, on May 14, 1976, by Ronald E. Marcello in Austin, Texas, North Texas State University, Oral History Collection, No. 322, "The Spirit of the *Arizona*," pp. 11–12.

The description of the burned men on the quarterdecks was from an interview with James Cory on December 21, 1976, by Ronald E. Marcello in Dallas, Texas, North Texas State University, Oral History Collection, No. 358, "The Spirit of the *Arizona*," p. 93.

The eyewitness account of the *Arizona* exploding is from an interview with Martin Matthews, August 2, 1978, by Ronald E. Marcello in Richardson, Texas, North Texas State University, Oral History Collection, No. 430, p. 31.

The details about the debris from the *Arizona* raining down on other ships in the harbor is from Prange, *At Dawn We Slept,* p. 514.

The eyewitness account of the debris raining down on our ship is from an interview with Martin Matthews, August 2, 1978, by Ronald E. Marcello in Richardson, Texas, North Texas State University, Oral History Collection, No. 430, p. 32.

The description of the men on the quarterdeck was from an interview with Clay H. Musick, on May 14, 1976, by Ronald E. Marcello in Austin, Texas, North Texas State University, Oral History Collection, No. 322, "The Spirit of the *Arizona,*" p. 11. The words of Earl Pecotte and Edward Wentzlaff about Lieutenant Commander Fuqua are from Slackman, *Remembering Pearl Harbor,* p. 121.

Fuqua went on to serve with distinction for the duration of the war on the USS *Tuscaloosa,* where he served as operations officer for the Seventh Fleet. He helped plan and execute several amphibious landings on the islands of the Philippines and of Borneo. He received the Congressional Medal of Honor for his valor on December 7, 1941. He retired from active service in July 1953. He died on January 27, 1987, and he was buried with full military honors at Arlington National Cemetery. The incident of Don and five of his shipmates being rescued by the line that was tied from the *Arizona* to the *Vestal* was documented in Joy Waldron Jasper, James P. Delgado, and Jim Adams, *The USS* Arizona: *The Ship, the Men, the Pearl Harbor Attack, and the Symbol That Aroused America* (New York: St. Martin's Press, 2001), p. 153.

The incident of Don and five of his shipmates being rescued by Joe George was corroborated by an eyewitness on the *Vestal*, Frank L. Dolan, who was interviewed on August 2, 1978, by Ronald E. Marcello in Richardson, Texas, North Texas State University, Oral History Collection, No. 430, p. 35.

5: The Damage

Confirmation of the death of Admiral Isaac C. Kidd is in Joy Waldron Jasper, James P. Delgado, and Jim Adams, *The USS* Arizona: *The Ship, the Men, the Pearl Harbor Attack, and the Symbol That Aroused America* (New York: St. Martin's Press, 2001), p. 13.

The story of the diver finding his friend is from Henry Berry, *"This Is No Drill!": Living Memories of the Attack on Pearl Harbor* (New York: Berkley, 1992), p. 157.

The description of Sterling Cale's work was found in Thurston Clarke, *Pearl Harbor Ghosts: The Legacy of December 7, 1941* (New York: Ballantine, 1991), pp. 134–35.

The experience of one of the divers doing salvage work on the *Arizona* was found in Berry, *"This Is No Drill!,"* p. 172.

For a graphic account from a Navy diver assigned the task of recovering bodies from the *"Arizona"* and other ships in the harbor, see the book by Edward C. Raymer, *"Descent into Darkness: Pearl Harbor, 1941: A Navy Diver's Memoir.* Annapolis, Maryland.

6: Among Angels

The quote at the beginning of the chapter is from a report by Navy Medical Department Preparedness, December 1941.

The reference to the boat from the hospital ship *Solace* rescuing men from the flaming waters around the *Arizona* was taken from the Annual Sanitary Report from the Base Force, Pacific Fleet, 1941.

The reference about the correlation between the severity of the burns and the amount of the clothing worn is from "Some Observations on the Casualties at Pearl Harbor," *Naval Medical Bulletin,* vol. 40, No. 2, pp. 353–58; "The SOLACE in action," *Naval Medical Bulletin,* vol. 40, No. 3, pp. 552–57; annual sanitary report for 1941 from the Base Force, Pacific Fleet; medical officer in command of Naval Hospital, Pearl Harbor, to Chief of Bureau of Navigation, 22, Dec. 1941; Ravdin-Long report.

The recollections from Rosella Asbelle came from the U.S. Navy Medical Department Oral History Program. Oral History with Lt. (ret) Rosella Asbelle, NC, USN, conducted by Jan K. Herman, 13 June 2002. Telephonic interview. Office of Medical History Bureau of Medicine and Surgery, 2300 E Street, NW, Washington, D.C. 20372.

The quote about boys becoming men is from Blake Clark, *Remember Pearl Harbor* (New York: Harper & Brothers, 1942), p. 135.

The figures for those treated at the Naval Hospital came from the Ravdin-Long report, derived from a letter by the medical officer in command of the Naval Hospital, Pearl Harbor, December 19, 1941.

The midnight bed count at the hospital on December 7, 1941, came from a letter from the medical officer in command of the hospital to the commandant of the fourteenth Naval District, December 19, 1941.

The comment about the calmness and courtesy in the hospital is from Clarke, *Remember Pearl Harbor,* pp. 134–35.

The statement about most of the men experiencing shock in some degree is from a memorandum on Dental Corps at Pearl Harbor by D. C. Emerson, December 7, 1941; December 15, 1941; medical officer in command of Naval Hospital, Pearl Harbor, to Chief of Bureau of Medicine and Surgery, January 16, 1942; Ravin-Long report.

The observations from the doctors who treated burn patients is from "Some Observations on the Casualties at Pearl Harbor," *Naval Medical Bulletin* 40, no. 2 (1942): 353–58; "The SOLACE in Action," *Naval Medical Bulletin* 40, no. 3 (1942): 552–57; annual sanitary report for 1941 from the Base Force, Pacific Fleet; medical officer in command of Naval Hospital, Pearl Harbor, to Chief of the Bureau of Navigation, December 22, 1941; Ravdin-Long report.

The account of blood donors was corroborated by Clarke, *Remember Pearl Harbor,* pp. 155–58.

The commendation of the ladies of Hotel Street was from the book, "Hotel Street Harry." Highland Park, Illinois: RTC Publishing , 2016, pp. 3-4.

7: America Responds

The quote that opens the chapter is from Dan van der Vat, *Pearl Harbor: The Day of Infamy—An Illustrated History* (New York: Basic Books, 2001), p. 154.

The quote by the gunner's mate is from Thurston Clarke, *Pearl Harbor Ghosts: The Legacy of December 7, 1941* (New York: Ballantine, 1991), p. 217.

The shortages listed can be found in Craig Shirley, "The Eighth of December," in *December 1941: 31 Days that Changed America and Saved the World* (Nashville, TN: Thomas Nelson, 2011), pp. 183–208, *passim.*

The portion of FDR's address that is quoted is from File No. 1401-A, December 9, 1941, Fireside Chat No. 18—re: War with Japan.

8: Recovery

The quote at the beginning of the chapter is from Stanley Weintraub, *Pearl Harbor Christmas: A World at War, December 1941* (Boston: Da Capo Press, 2011), p. 85.

FDR's words about us all being the United States of America is from his fireside chat on April 28, 1942, "On Our Economic Policy."

9: Home to Red Cloud

The quote at the beginning of the chapter is from Thomas Wolfe, *You Can't Go Home Again* (New York: Scribner, 2011), p. 50.

The quote that begins, "You can't go home to your family . . ." is from Wolfe, *You Can't Go Home Again,* p. 602.

10: Back in the Fight

The quote at the beginning of the chapter is from William Shakespeare, *Henry V,* "St. Crispin's Day Speech," Act 4, Scene 3. Folger Shakespeare Library, Washington Square Press, 2004.

The quote from Admiral Turner is from the book by Robin L. Rielly, "Kamikazes, Corsairs, and Picket Ships:" Okinawa, 1945. Havertown, Pennsylvania: Casemate Publishers, 2008, p. 348.

11: Endgame

The quote at the beginning of the chapter is from a speech Roosevelt had been scheduled to give on Jefferson Day, April 13, 1945, the day after his death.

The words of Roosevelt about making the world safe for our children are from his fireside chat, "On War with Japan," December 9, 1945.

The two quotes from David Brooks are from his book *The Road to Character* (New York: Random House, 2015), pp. 3–4.

The quote by Truman on the language of bombardment is from John W. Dower, *Cultures of War: Pearl Harbor, Hiroshima, 9–11, Iraq* (New York: Norton, 2010), p. 279.

MacArthur's words are from a book by Bill Sloan, "The Ultimate Battle:" Okinawa 1945—The Last Epic Struggle of World War II. New York: Simon & Schuster Paperbacks, 2007, pp. 351–352.

12: The Lessons of Pearl Harbor

The quote at the beginning of the chapter is from Franklin D. Roosevelt, fireside chat, "On War with Japan," December 9, 1941.

The war warning to General Short is from Gordon W. Prange with Donald M. Goldstein and Katherine V. Dillon, *Pearl Harbor: The Verdict of History* (New York: McGraw-Hill, 1986), p. 720.

The war warning to Admiral Kimmel is from Prange, *Pearl Harbor: The Verdict of History,* p. 721.

The conversation between Morgan and Kimmel is documented in John W. Dower, *Cultures of War: Pearl Harbor, Hiroshima, 9–11, Iraq* (New York: Norton, 2010), p. 43.

13: Remembering the *Arizona*

The quote at the beginning of the chapter is from Gordon W. Prange with Donald M. Goldstein and Katherine V. Dillon, *Pearl Harbor: The Verdict of History* (New York: McGraw-Hill, 1986), p. 629.

The diary entry by President Bush is from John W. Dower, *Cultures of War: Pearl Harbor, Hiroshima, 9–11, Iraq* (New York: Norton, 2010), p. 4.

A picture of the plaque given to the memorial by the United Japanese Society of Hawaii is in Michael Slackman, *Remembering Pearl Harbor: The Story of the USS* Arizona *Memorial* (Honolulu: *Arizona* Memorial Museum Association, 1984), p. 82.

My memories of the *Arizona* Memorial, which I have visited fifteen times, have been sharpened by Slackman, *Remembering Pearl Harbor.*

The stories of the twenty-fifth and forty-fifth anniversaries of Pearl Harbor can be found in Thurston Clarke, *Pearl Harbor Ghosts: The Legacy of December 7, 1941* (New York: Ballantine, 1991), pp. 118–22. Mention of Don's story is on p. 121.

The passage about loving your enemies can be found in Matthew 5:43–48.

The passage about forgiving your enemies can be found in Mark 11:25.

The dedication and names of the dead that are etched in marble on the memorial wall were installed and rededicated by AMVETS on April 4, 1984.

The conversation between Kendall Fielder and Mitsuo Fuchida was from Clarke, *Pearl Harbor Ghosts,* pp. 120–21.

The conversations with Sterling Cale and his wife and Ray Emory and the author were from Clarke, *Pearl Harbor Ghosts,* p. 257.

The firsthand account of Mitsuo Fuchida's conversion is from Mitsuo Fuchida, *From Pearl Harbor to Calvary: True Story of the Lead Pilot of the Pearl Harbor Attack and His Conversion to Christianity* (Escondido, CA: eChristian, 2011). The book was originally published in 1953 under the title *From Pearl Harbor to Golgotha.*

A more detailed account of Mitsuo Fuchida's conversion is from Gordon W. Prange, with Donald M. Goldstein and Katherine V. Dillon, *God's Samurai: Lead Pilot at Pearl Harbor* (Washington, DC: Potomac Books, 2004). Prange was a professor of history at the University of Maryland and a Pearl Harbor scholar who wrote two definitive books on the subject: *At Dawn We Slept: The Untold Story of Pearl Harbor,* and *Pearl Harbor: The Verdict of History.* During the course of his research, Prange consulted Fuchida over the years, and the two of them eventually became good friends.

14: Preparing for the Seventy-Fifth Anniversary

The quote about life ending is from Thomas Wolfe, *You Can't Go Home Again* (New York: Scribner, 2011), p. 638.

For a schedule of events for the seventy-fifth anniversary of Pearl Harbor, see http://www.pearlharbor75thanniversary.com. For information about tours: http://www.beyondbandofbrothers.com and http://www.enoa.com. For symposiums: http://www.Pearl75.org.

Epilogue: Preparing for Heaven

The quote at the beginning of the Epilogue is from the film *Saving Private Ryan,* 1998, DreamWorks, directed by Steven Spielberg.

The story about the rabbi and the woman is by Rabbi Tzvi Freeman, "Memory and Loss." The rabbi is senior editor of Chabad.org and the author of *Bringing Heaven Down to Earth* (Holbrook, MA: Adams Media, 1999).

Index